In the Heart
of the Heart
of Another Country

In the Heart
of the Heart
of Another Country

Etel Adnan

City Lights Books
San Francisco

Cover design: Yolanda Montijo
Cover photograph: Pirkle Jones
Typography: Harvest Graphics
Editor: Nancy J. Peters

Library of Congress Cataloging-in-Publication Data

Adnan, Etel.
   In the heart of the heart of another country / Etel Adnan.
      p.   cm.

   ISBN-10: 0-87286-446-4
1. Beirut (Lebanon)—Poetry.   2. California—Poetry.
   I. Title.   II. Series.
   PS3551.D65148 2005
   811'.54—dc22

                                                    2005007523

CITY LIGHTS BOOKS are edited by Lawrence Ferlinghetti
and Nancy J. Peters and published at the City Lights
Bookstore, 261 Columbus Avenue, San Francisco CA 94133.
www.citylights.com

ACKNOWLEDGMENTS

Grateful acknowledgment is given to the following journals and books, where the following texts were first published.

Mundus Artium, University of Texas Press at Dallas, 1977 ("In the Heart of the Heart of Another Country"); *First Intensity*, Fall 1998 ("At Both Ends"); *Penumbra*, University of California at Stanislaus, 1999 ("Twenty-five Years Later"); *Archipelago*, vol. 4 ("Further On"); www.blithe.com, winter, 2004 ("Time, Desire and Fog"); and *War & Peace; an Anthology*, edited by Leslie Scalapino, O Books, 2004 (the first part of "To Be In a Time of War").

To Ronald Vance
& George Deem

CONTENTS

INTRODUCTION

by Etel Adnan

It was on a soft San Francisco morning, sometime in 1971, that I picked up at City Lights Bookstore a copy of William H. Gass's remarkable collection of stories titled *In the Heart of the Heart of the Country*. I went home and started to read the book. The piece that gave its name to the book is not a story in the ordinary sense. It engages the reader immediately with a series of paragraphs, or sections, each with a heading that sometimes recurs, but often does not. It made a powerful impression on me.

A year later I left California and moved back to Lebanon, where I was born. The return stirred all kinds of conflicting feelings. When I left home, I had thought that it was forever, and now I was returning after having spent seventeen years in the San Francisco Bay Area, and thinking I would resettle for good in Beirut.

William H. Gass starts his story by telling that he was "returning to B . . . ." He continues paragraph after paragraph, each headed with a recurring word or phrase, to build a kind of a provincial city that gradually acquires the quality of a quasi-mythical place.

Beirut was then *the* mythical city of the world. That was the way it was. It was also something else. Life was exciting, truly, but also painful. Painful may not necessarily be the right word; the reality of Beirut was of a complexity defying definition.

My new life as a cultural journalist was going in all directions, as was the city itself. Beirut stood at the core of the

Arab World, and sheltered the headquarters of all the information-gathering agencies known on the map. It was a refuge for all sorts of political opponents to the various governments in the region, and the matrix for all the tensions that were tearing the world apart. This reverberated in the minds of everybody living there and created, under a skin of glamour, a ruthless cynicism that would be justified, only a few years later, by the tremendous explosion whose energy required more than fifteen years of fighting to be spent. Civil War was brewing, and many were already aware of the man-made earthquake that was soon to engulf everything.

Political theories had been debated ad infinitum and ad nauseam. The line between James Bond–style movies and the surrealistic cruelty of international manipulations was erased. The cabarets had an air of do-or-die, the very atmosphere that precedes unintended catastrophes. In that whirlwind, any living body, human or animal, looked fragile, and that sentiment of precariousness had narrowed the realm of my interests to the myriad little happenings that were crowding my mind. Contrary to what is usually believed, it is not general ideas and a grandiose unfolding of great events that most impress the mind in times of heightened historical upheavals but, rather, it is the uninterrupted flow of little experiences, observations, disturbances, small ecstasies, or barely perceptible discouragements that make up the trivialized day-to-day living.

Seldom have I had the feeling, as I did then, that I was a small fish capable of witnessing only miniscule—though enlarged—images of very troubled waters.

One does not return to one's country of origin after a long absence without bringing back some glory, and some damage. I was constantly alarmed by what I was perceiving in an environment both old and new to me. California was on my mind, working like a filtering device. My references belonged to two worlds, and were forcing me to shift gears, so to speak, to be mobile, edgy, and, most of all, vulnerable. I was used to a world now remote and, at the same time, getting used to a new one that was also my old world, and somewhere, deep inside, I was alien to both.

I was not thinking about writing, or painting, too busy with a new job and a new society, in an overheated frenetic city seized by monstrous and driving passions that were pushing it to its death. One day, though, some bitter questions took hold of me. What did I leave behind? And what did I find in this land whose antiquity was deeply buried and was now manifesting layers of violence, transience, and madness?

I recalled William Gass's piece, the world he was depicting, which seemed at this point unreachable and peaceful. I entered into silent conversation with him, his story. As I reread it, the paragraphs jumped off of the page as if addressed to me, asking for a response. I thought along these lines: So you are in America, and I am here; you may think that you're in trouble, or that there's trouble in your country, but come here and see for yourself the mire into which we're sinking. Just look.

I must confess that have always felt a particular attraction to paragraphs, especially when they happen to be headed by a single word. Personal history is involved: In the little classrooms of the neighborhood school that I attended as a child, the days were usually neither dull nor exciting. They just passed by. It was a routine, interrupted by regular recreation breaks, the only times I eagerly awaited. But there was, for some years in a row, something very special, unforgettable, the memory of which still acts on me: our weekly composition assignment. Our teacher, a nun in Catholic elementary school, would give us a few words, and we had to write a sentence using them.

This pleasure in writing that I experienced intensely in those days remains as the memory of an addiction, and once in a while it recurs as I work; and I can wait months or years for it to happen again the way it was back then. While we were to write one sentence around a given word, I would write a whole paragraph, or even more. I remember most vividly the state of mind, a state of trance. Bent over the wooden desk, my head almost touching its surface, I was writing sentences in a flow, hypnotized. I still look for moments like those. There's a kind of "rightness" there, like that which sailors feel when they reach the ecstatic moment of their cruising speed, when the smooth sailing on a sea merges with desire and becomes pure revelation.

The simple words chosen seemingly at random by Gass *had* to stir the deepest layers of my soul, carrying me back to the school assignments, to that sheer happiness residing between somnolence and voyage. I began by taking over his headings and "answering" them. They became magic keys, no longer to the *B. . . .* that was his city in his country, but to the city of Beirut, a harbor in Lebanon. And so I went about telling *my side* of the story, entering into the heart of the heart of *another* country. . . . Eventually, the piece appeared in *Mundus Artium* in Texas, and I went on with other projects and activities.

One day, I was asked to contribute to the literary magazine *Penumbra*, in a special issue featuring Bay Area poets and writers. I said yes. Then quite by chance I happened to pull out that old issue of *Mundus Artium*, dormant in my bookshelves, and instantly decided to go back to the format of my story. This was twenty-five years later! I felt driven to the same headings of paragraphs that were, by now of course, arousing responses different from the initial ones.

Subsequently, but at considerably smaller intervals, I wrote three more works in the same vein: "Further On," "Present Time," and "Time, Desire and Fog." One can say that the whole endeavor was close to writing an autobiography, the past mixing with the present, each distorting the other, opening into the tensions of repetition. A cycle was formed, comprising two currents: on the one hand, the recurring key words that established an anchor as if given by destiny; and on the other, the responses, the paragraphs going their own chaotic ways. I was returning again and again to the heart of the matter, and each time the heart was changing, had changed. It was exhilarating.

"Time, Desire and Fog" grew out of my recent discovery that in ancient times the first deities of Sidon were the entities Time, Desire, and Fog. The discovery made me dreamy, all the more because I would have never associated the archetypal city of Sidon (called Sayda today) with fog. But after a trip there, those three deities, taken together, fit perfectly into the general atmosphere of the feelings and imaginings that led to the writing of that story.

At some point, the cycle of five affiliated though separate pieces attracted into their orbit two other works: "At Both Ends" and "To Be in a Time of War."

"At Both Ends," the piece about T. E. Lawrence, was written in the last month of the last century, while I was assessing the disasters that stand out as milestones in our lives. For the Arab East, the 20th century started in turmoil, and with hope: the desire to break away from the Ottoman Empire and start an era of independence. The Arabs were soon to be betrayed and, seen from our end, their history has been regularly marked with series of betrayals, as if to betray one's lesser allies has to be, for the West, customary policy.

The most famous Western figure of the tragedy of betrayal, in this case a tragedy for both the agent and the victim, is certainly Lawrence. Once I had the waking dream that he was still in the process of writing *The Seven Pillars of Wisdom* as the policies he served and the disasters that they brought about are continuing to this hour. These disasters are a permanent landscape against which everything in that part of the world has to be measured.

I identified with his story both as an Arab and a non-Arab, taking the risk of sharing an Orientalist's vision. In fact, I was neither one in this particular case. I was mainly trying to give flesh and bones to the notion of betrayal, a look at history through a particular life and a particular place: the one gone, and the other disappearing. I was clearing my mind like somebody cleans out his drawers. Lawrence is no more. The century is gone. And with all efforts made into turning deserts into tourist ventures, there are, for the imagination at least, no more virgin territories left. The deserts of the 21st century are already Moon and Mars.

The emblematic image of Lawrence called me, like some words do, because they have a charge that forces the mind to look through them the way one uses special lenses for some special research. And the question of betrayal, so tied to his image, is a crucial one: ultimately, of all the betrayals the most damaging to the mind and to the heart is the betrayal of one's own self.

In March 2003, war was brewing in Iraq. History was again bringing unbearable tensions. My imagination was on fire and my anger was increased by the triumphant tone of the news. In California, very few people were really concerned. Few had ever been to Iraq, and fewer were those ready to consider the destruction of Iraq in terms of human and cultural loss. I was numb with apprehension, and it happened that at some moment, sitting at my table, detached from my environment, projected to an East of my own mind, and alienated from myself, I took paper and ink and started to write "To Be in a Time of War."

I IN THE HEART OF THE HEART OF ANOTHER COUNTRY

PLACE

So I have sailed the seas and come . . .

to B . . .

a city by the sea, in Lebanon. It is seventeen years later. My absence has been an exile from an exile. I'm of those people who are always doing what somebody else is doing . . . but a few weeks earlier. A fish in a warm sea. No house for shelter, but a bed, from house to house, and clothes crumpled on a single shelf. I am searching for love.

WEATHER

In Beirut there is one season and a half. Often, the air is still. I get up in the morning and breathe heavily. The winter is damp. My bones ache. I have a neighbor who spits blood when at last it rains.

MY HOUSE

My father built a house when I was a child near the German school so I could go to it. The school moved out as he finished the roof. Ever since, my property has been rented for the cheapest rent in town. The laws are such that I can't push out the tenants. Anyway, I am afraid of houses as of tombs.

A PERSON

My other neighbor (from neighbor to neighbor I shall cover the world) sells birds. And cats. A Siamese cat was born, and it was really Siamese: it had two heads, four ears, two bodies, two sets of four legs, two tails. My neighbor has on sale a little monkey, which has been growing for the last seventeen and half years. The store is in front of a newspaper that went broke. Since, all the windows are blind.

WIRES
They are few, and, as there are no trees in Beirut, the wirepoles are dead, geometric semblances of trees. Dead archetypes. As for the birds, Lebanese hunters have killed them all. Now they are killing the Syrian birds, too.

THE CHURCH
We have churches, mosques, and synagogues. All equally empty at night. On weekends, many flies desert their gardens. People come in.

MY HOUSE
I should say my side of the bed. Half a bed makes a big house at night. My dreams have the power to extend space and make me live in the greatest mansions. During the day it doesn't matter. There are many streets, a few remaining sidewalks, and, yes, the Café Express in which I move, hunted by memories.

POLITICS
Oh, it's too much, too much. Once I dreamed of becoming the new Ibn Khaldoun of America or the de Tocqueville of the Arabs. Now I work for a newspaper and cover the most menial things. So I don't understand how it is that there are kings without kingdoms and Palestinians without a Palestine. As for the different scandals, they do not matter to me. Why should I care that some thieves steal from other thieves. Should I?

PEOPLE
The Lebanese go on two feet, like the Chinese for example; sometimes, on four, to pick up a dime under the table. Their country is small, their desires too, and their love affairs. Only their cars are big. Detroit made Chevys and Buicks. All

the unsold Buicks of America are on our roads. So, in this country, you only see the heads of the people. Their bodies are carefully washed and stored away. As for the women, there aren't any. They all consider themselves as being the other half of their men. With one exception.

VITAL DATA
The most interesting things in Beirut are the absent ones. The absence of an opera house, of a football field, of a bridge, of a subway, and, I was going to say, of the people and of the government. And, of course, the absence of absence of garbage.

EDUCATION
Everybody speaks Arabic, French, English, Armenian, Greek and Kurdish. Sometimes one language at a time, sometimes all of them together. And even the children are financiers.

BUSINESS
Merchants sell to other merchants and buy from them. Men sell women to other men and buy women from them. Women sell women to women. And everybody sells a child: for vanity, for money, for pleasure. In the tall buildings of Hamra children get assaulted under the eyes of their parents. Parents thank God when they get the money.

MY HOUSE, THIS PLACE AND BODY
There was a house in a eucalyptus grove. My father and I sneaked in, and in the middle of the night a guard came to awaken us. I advised my father to offer him money and he did: he gave him 900 pounds. "I didn't ask for that much," said the guard. My father, then, disappeared.

Don't talk to me about my body. It has been battered, cut open; discs, nerves, and tissues have been removed. My belly, a zoological garden. My eyes, poor lighthouses, and my mind a rocky and barren garden, exactly like this place and the nonexistent house.

(3)

THE SAME PERSON

I went to the store, and, feeling sorry for the caged birds, I told the guy: "How can you sell animals?" He replied: "Aren't you an animal too?" So I lowered my eyes and admired him.

WEATHER

I used to love the heat, and, even now, the sweat. My sheets used to get wet and I, rolling in them, my body in ecstasy. I was then sixteen, or a bit more. I kissed the air of this town with passion and carried it in my arms. I couldn't love a man because I loved the sea. Then, I went away, and the spell broke. The weather aged, got wrinkles, its bones and marrow became soft. It is nowadays like breathing mud. When it rains, I can't feel happy for the trees. They do not exist. So I feel happy for the buildings. They get an imperfect bath. As for me, the eternal sun has worked like a siren on my brain.

It has eaten up my intelligence. The dust has filled my nails. Cockroaches run over my paintings, and I get up at night to kill them and to keep them away at the edge of my dream. But the dampness is constant, and invisible amoebae constantly dance in the air. One feels always a bit swollen in Beirut. It is a pregnancy of bad omen. You have to go to a village called Sannine to start breathing properly. But you never stay too long up there. You miss the weather of Beirut.

PLACE

I left this place by running all the way to California. An exile, which lasted for years. I came back on a stretcher and felt here a stranger, exiled from my former exile. I am always away from something and somewhere. My senses left me one by one to have a life of their own. If you meet me in the street, don't be sure it is me. My center is not in the solar system.

PEOPLE

This is the cruelest place. A man in a motorboat hit a swimmer and sped away. The skull was broken. A large space of blood covered the sea. Painters rushed to the scene to make a painting for sale. A girl was killed by her brother because she smiled to her lover. A house in the city was set on fire because they wanted the tenants out. A rebellion has started, the rebellion of the rich against the poor. Yes, to make sure that the latter do not multiply; rather, that they be dead, and the sooner the better.

MY HOUSE MY CAT MY COMPANY

From every drawer, the blood of my spirit is spilled. My eyes, anguished by the light, have cruel particles of dust covering them. Noises come in as demons. No crime in the newspaper is as gory as the noises that surround my bed. It is an eternal beat.

Mao is the name of my cat, who has been rescued from a friend. He sleeps on my left side, watches my heartbeats. At night, when he sometimes runs away, I have to go out and look for him. Most often, he runs out at about four in the morning, when the Koranic prayer fills the air, and when its lamentation seems endless and fills me with sacred terror. That terror is communicated somehow to Mao whose hair stands up. He shivers against me when we come home.

One morning my breast was bare and he put his paw on it. It was a moment of perfection.

So I gave him away, but he came back.

I live with a woman who shares my passion for ants, from the day I told her that my father had taught me to watch them attentively in order to imitate them later in life. This was my education. I was told that ants had all the necessary qualities; they were tiny and carried weights bigger than their size. They never slept. Industrious, they stuck together, never doing anything alone. And when you killed them, they multiplied. So my friend fell in love with my father for having been so right. But he is dead. The ants keep me company, coming from under the flower pots all the way into the closets, glasses, spoons. They stop at the door of the refrigerator. Their brain is tinier than the head of a pin. So angels must exist.

I am a species all by myself. That's why no fish comes to swim in my territorial waters. I have no enemies.

I live with a woman who has a recurring dream: each night she goes to unearth Akhnaton and carries his coffin all over the house. The young king has a nocturnal journey in her arms. His solar boat had been shattered by his murderers. She weeps for him, sometimes, during the day too, but she does not go around like the women from America in pink slippers and bobby pins to the supermarket. No. She uses silverware, puts salt and pepper on her meat, and she tells me that she does not proceed from a source of light but from a source of shadows.

As for me, I told her that I find my reason to be in the configurations of matter.

I love with violence the different objects I encounter. I have a passion for cars. My spoon is to me what the angel used to be to Jacob: my moment of truth. People throw their fingernails away, and I look at these pieces of matter with awe: transparent like alabaster, tiny like African ants, pale as erased memories. I throw them away with a tremendous melancholy. I would like to be buried with "Saint James Infirmary" playing. Or something like that, maybe a song by Oum Kalsoum.

Then I would like to resurrect. Death would appear as short as the time for the batting of an eyelash. I am of those who like resurrection, and I am not alone in that; I hear people saying it, when I walk, and mostly in New York.

POLITICS
The State. A man and a woman, together, already form a state. There is everything between them: a principle of

authority, a government, laws of behavior, embassy and representation, diplomacy, weapons, periods of peace and war. They also constitute, to make things harder than for matters of state, two different species. When they meet, they sometimes ignore each other. Sometimes, they climb on each other like a pair of monkeys. At other times, a current of cool air passes from the one to the other: there is love. And then, there are times when, at their contact, a short-circuit happens, and they burn each other and leave nothing behind them but a spot on the sun.

Youssef el Khal said one day that I was a poet. Yes. I am the poet in the heart of the city. A dot. I am the poet of the here and now.

But, being a woman, I am invisible. I have to hide my obsession for ants. They pursue me. If a woman went to the marketplace and cried for help because ants were climbing up her legs, some men would throw themselves between her thighs and search wildly for the tiny beasts in order to relieve her from her fear, and to hurt her too. But she would be arrested and thrown into an insane asylum until she hallucinated and the water that fell from the faucet became a thick stream of black ants. In that case, I would pull up my blanket of flies and sleep.

MORE VITAL DATA
Like a salmon, I came back here to die. But this place is not a place. I am unable to die.

By a big dam on the Columbia River I saw a salmon swim upstream and break itself on the concrete slopes of the dam. The large Columbia River is a stream that makes its mark on the universe.

If I came to Beirut from that far away, it is to bemoan the Pacific. My passion is for the beach. Pisces-born, I am the Indian salmon originating in an Arab land.

In Hamra street, in Bourj and Bab Edriss, people are breathing gasoline, and they like it; it is still cheaper than water in a country of drought.

EDUCATION
Children are taught that little boys are superior to little girls. Yes. When Hassan beats Nedjma, Nedjma is beaten by her father for having been beaten, and this, ad infinitum . . .

And nobody ever tells them, oh never! that a rat is as human as a cat. And the slow process of castration starts on the wooden benches of the classrooms. We need schools without walls. We need to be a nation of swimmers. We need the end of nations. The end of ends.

In this avaricious country, even the moon looks like a coin, because children are taught numbers. As for me, I learned arithmetic by killing ants and counting their dead little bodies.

BUSINESS
This place is a crossroad with no red lights. A station for outer spacemen. An immigration point. Look how they come from Jupiter and Mars, the colonizers. I used to go walking from Damascus to Rakka under a forest of apricot trees. But trade moved in and the forest disappeared.

I already told you that a bottle of water is more expensive than a bottle of gasoline. So, let us drink oil. We buy mirrors and drugs, but we do not have the funeral parlors of America and the Jewish barbershops of Tel Aviv. No. Business is healthy. It is all a traffic of toys bought always with somebody else's sweat. And then there is the airport. It brings in millions of dollars, It takes out millions of people. The biggest business in town is to carry baggage, back and forth. Buy your ticket to the moon and we will carry your slippers free. Buy. Buy. Buy.

THAT SAME PERSON

Because I told him a rat is as human as a cat, he threw himself on me and said he had to talk. We went together into the prostitution quarter of the city. "I can't talk unless I play a bit before," he said, so we went into a store and took rifles and shot at moving targets. He pulled down two stuffed bears. We went to have dinner. He told me: "Don't let them get me. In Kabul they wanted to put me in prison, and I fled. You don't know what they do to prisoners there. They keep them in a well where water reaches their belt. A man who was a former ambassador stayed in there three years. He has never been the same.

"The American in whose house Timothy Leary was arrested was put for five months into that well. He came out insane. His wife was put into a big hole with no water and with open skies, but the guards were forbidden to come too close to the hole so that they would not rape her and the other women. They had, therefore, to throw the food to them as to beasts. But these women have a memory."

Right in front of the restaurant was Marika's house. We came up to the three story house, and he said hello to her and then kissed her Muslim friend, Afaf, on the forehead. Marika has the gentleness of the typical Greek prostitute in an Arab harbor. We ran down the stairs. Two Lebanese soldiers were looking for the door. They made an indecent gesture. He laughed. He was perspiring more and more and he said: "I want to talk about the ultimate, next to a fan." We found a little cafe, with a table with a marble top and iron legs, drank some water, and started an infinite conversation about his desire for little girls.

WIRES

The thread of this century is made of wire. German camps, surrounded by wire and spikes, all over Europe and in Greece. . . . British wires in Egypt. Israeli wires in Palestine and on the southern border of Lebanon. People's mouths sewn with wires and Che Guevara's body bandaged with them and dragged from one place to another. A Viet Cong hanged not by rope but by iron. All the little electric wires which criss-cross my brain, attaching in an imperfect way one thought to another, my hunger to my exile, and my body to this place. Each one of us is a dog attached by steel threads to a purpose, waiting for lightning to strike.

WEATHER
Spring is deadly, like red roses.

The weather always awakens in me the fear of death. I am of those animals who have a strong life instinct, but the forces of death, like huge tides, beat against me. I go from country to country and each time, the earth, under my feet, becomes an ocean. So I move on. Chasing each place's weather.

At noon, I visit buildings under construction, I look at the Syrian workers while they eat. There is always some cement on their bread. When they cut a watermelon, they count the black seeds in order to know how many days separate them from their own death. They don't know what they are doing. It is for them like playing chess.

Spring starts, here, in February. We faint at our desks. In classrooms. In rooms. A thin veil of sweat covers my face and my neck, runs between my shoulders, all along my spine. My nerves quiver. The heat grows. In June, July, August, I resemble a flat tire. Then, all kinds of amoebae stir in my belly. The heat is a culture bed, my body works like marshes, and in the green foliage of my insides flowers of sonic anti-paradise grow. Airplanes zoom above, and, because I am a four-footed animal, I stay on the ground, and even below. October in Beirut is the end of the road to hell. Dampness has reached its saturation point. By then one can hardly move. Tired bones, tired eyes, tired fingers. One by one my nerves go. The harbor is cluttered. So are the streets. In a dark and polluted air I act as if I were breathing. The year is almost gone, and the very short rains are waiting.

PLACE

My place is at the center of things. I am writing from within the nucleus of an atom. Blood beating in my ears. Dry heat radiating from my nerves. A pressure trying to push my eyes ahead of me; they want to travel on their own. My place: highways, trains, cars. One road after another, from ocean shore to ocean shore. From Beirut to the Red Sea. From Aden to Algiers. From Oregon to La Paz. I keep going, prisoner of a body, and my brain is just a radio station emitting messages to outer space. Angels, astronauts all dressed in white, I would like some strange being to take me somewhere where no disease blurs my perception. I will grow wings and fly.

PEOPLE

Charlie Mingus came to Baalbeck. They loved him. He behaved like a bird. Huge, with shining copper wings. He turned the air into a jungle. They danced. They expanded their bodies. They grew feathers, horns, antlers, spikes, teeth.

In the morning they all went to the small cages they call their offices. Some of them made telephone calls.

But look, I want a revolution. I go through the daydreams. Women don't make war or peace. Neither do the men. There is also a long line of ants waiting for their turn. They want to form a new government; they can't. Some higher insects have reached their nervous system and paralyzed their will.

Arab women form a people of their own. A poorly run secret society. They are trying hard but do it in confusion. They are at their best on television. Men have never looked at them. Looked at them the way you look at the sunset.

So the cameras, once in a while, come to these women. Beasts with round eyes who throw their ray-like desires upon them. The women know that at last after trillions of years they are being looked at: their eyes meet the eyes of

(11)

the camera, an icy love affair. They stand alone, face-to-face. The room is dark. The darkness removes the edges of the studio. So it is similar to being in the universe.

Flashlights drill their way into their souls; it makes them feel they are a target. Deep inside, light uses its rays like a broom. It cleanses the inner soul piece by piece. At the end, all the plasma of birth is gone. Something bare has appeared, and the woman is terrified by such a reduction by search and fire.

So the thing goes on . . .

One being escaped the total fate of Arab women: Oum Kalsoum. When the Arabs were thinking that they had nothing, they were saying that after all they had Oum Kalsoum and that, all by herself, she represented their will to be, the religious essence of their culture; she pulled to herself, by the quality of her voice and the tone of each one of her words, the human tide that was coming toward her. This human tide became the tide of history, the tide of all the frustrations transfigured in a kind of bliss.

She sings "on target," like a whip to whatever in each one of us is dormant. And also, we can't forget it, a whip against anything foreign, because, then, the foreigner was the colonizer. She took it on herself to tell the world that the Arab world existed.

To all those castrated by underdevelopment and occupation, she was saying that she loved them. She sings as for you alone, and in this love as deep as valleys and the ocean floor, the fellah and the prime minister found, each, what forgives all sins and recycles the son in the grace of the mother.

Erotic being, like the Sufis, she reconciled the flesh and the spirit. She has been this century's thread. I heard her when I was twelve in the Grand Theatre of Beirut. It was a beneficial trauma.

Then I followed her: in Cairo, where on the first Thursday of each month she made people leave home with a transistor radio, or they gathered at night in shops to listen to her in their long and white robes. Listening to her songs, which lasted for four or five hours, I heard the Nile moan and the human species give birth. In the divisions that break a world and make it explode, she was the unity we had.

I follow her in Cairo, for her death. On February 5, I go to her funeral. On the tent near the Omar Makram mosque, where the human river is going to flow behind her coffin, a huge picture of her has a green ribbon on which it is written that she is the martyr of divine love. Yes, the sky is light, cloudy. The people are coming from everywhere, and the noise is like trees in the wind. "La Illah illa Allah," says the crowd. The army was here, but it is gone. The people become the sea and engulf the body.

And it floats, the small coffin covered with an iridescent blue and green veil. The people possess her and in their collective memory they take her away like a pharaonic boat.

HOUSE, MY BREATH AND WINDOW

A house is a cage, a monument, the mausoleum of all travels, an observatory, the belly of one's mother. Mine is now full of windows, above a harbor. It is a worried object, trembling at night. It makes one feel insecure. Furniture in it comes and goes. It is not my house but my television's house. The world comes in through television and sits on my chairs. I am the guardian of all those invisible things. A poet is the one who mounts the guard over the inanimate objects of this world. And this explains how my breath is essential. Don't accuse me of copying God. There is an old account to settle between us. My breath gives life to plants and on a single occasion it resuscitated a donkey. I took the animal's sickness and gave him my health. This new house of mine is made of windows. Beirut's light comes in like a full malediction. White white is the sun. The whiteness of death.

POLITICS

In my view Yasser Arafat existed only on television. For the people, he was in New York. An Arab in New York spoke of Palestine. His gestures were those of an Indian Chief. He was the real leader of a real country. He was also the possible leader of a possible country. Angels covered with blood were flying in the American sky. New York is the deep canyon of the soul.

Meanwhile Beirut moans and burns. But not a single voice is to be heard on behalf of the torn muscles, blinded eyes, cigarette-burned faces, vertebrae broken with an axe . . . It is as if Beirut has become an anatomy treatise that one reads in some dark corner of hell.

FINAL VITAL DATA

On the way to extreme consciousness one encounters, like on a high road, pain. Then, one backs up, turns around, and goes home.

What we call a loss of memory, the impossibility to remember, is in fact an inner deafness, thinking being separated, by some kind of a curtain, from the inner ear; it is a power failure.

That is how I discovered writing with no alphabet. One sign after another. One wave length after another. The tall eucalyptus trees were the measure.

In anguish. Absence. The absence of Time. The clear look of the sea. The green eyes of the ocean. The red guts that the Pacific had. The warm breath of the wind. And the hour that was falling on the street under the balcony, like a rain, the laguna not moving. To hurt wherever something is alive.

The sun lives on an island in a celestial ocean. I go with an uncertain speed. I push a stone with my foot, and, rolling, it kills a passerby on the bottom of the ravine. I know it. I return to a terrace white with haggard colors. The sun remains on its island. At the top of a stairway sustained by a wall, a policeman appears, followed by a hospital attendant. The needle that the latter holds announces my torture.

A voice takes hold of the bottom of my feet, moves up along my legs, stops at my knees and bends them slowly, slides like a sail on the Nile along my spine and bursts into millions of cells of my brain. I am a magic box.

I have the sadness of a meteor. I count one sunset after another. I become the stem of a new tree battered with wounds on which birds come to hold their tribal councils. Fish in the morning, bird in the evening, tree all through the day, I am at night a river that is flowing north.

I also have to tell you: I am, each year, a year older. But there is a place in an anti-universe where I am, each year, a year younger. I love matter. I swim in atoms when I am in the sea. I get covered with sand on the beaches of the Pacific, and food, for me, is made of electric particles. I love the moon because it is cold and barren, and I love a warm bath, when I come back from it. I am of those who kiss the dust not by womanly obedience but because it is part of the earth. And the big, big, clouds, like candy, come down my throat. There is a secret about me: my mobility. I go always faster than I go. This is why I am such a stranger to myself.

EDUCATION

They teach the children to obey: it is a castration. They teach the children the names of cities that have disappeared: they make them love death. There should be only one school, the one where you learn the future . . . without even any students. Located in the guts of the species. Where you would say: "If you could step out of your mind and walk in the fields, what would you do?
"Nothing."
"What do you mean? If you could step out of your mind and walk in the fields, where would you go?"

(15)

"Nowhere."
"What do you mean?"
"I myself would like to know."

ANOTHER PERSON

There is for each one of us an enemy. It lives all around us and inhabits the body. John has his own: it is his mother. He is sitting in the immense garden full of rubber trees and under hanging roots which belongs to his wife's family, and he compares it to an American Southern mansion.

It is hot, and it is night. We speak of the civil war. Everyone digs into his memory to bring out what is most painful. John speaks of his mother's death. He received her in the mail, incinerated and put into a plastic box. "I didn't know what to do with her," he said, "when she arrived that way in New York. I did not know any funeral rite. I had to invent one. I drew flowers on the little box that I did not dare open, and I put it in the garbage."

My enemy is Zamil. His name can also mean that he is a friend. Blue-eyed Arab, hawk-like, I see him on the top of the armoire. Sometimes he smokes a mixture of opium and aspirin. He also looks like my father when he was taking a bath, all covered with soap, slippery, unattainable. We go swimming together, make love under the waves. I am an amoeba in the dark aquarium which is the city, reaching for acids, stretching and shrinking. I am a fish. My scales rub against the top of the buildings and get torn. My gills absorb all the oil that there is in the water. I keep coming to the surface, but the sky is absent.

It is here, in this water, not in heaven, that my enemy lives. He is not even a person; often, he is but the passage of time. Beirut is too busy to know the beauty of the sea. It is also too cruel. The cruellest town in the world. This is why it, too, becomes my enemy.

THE FIRST PERSON

Is she another person? That enemy of mine has no face, no name, no being. Not even some shadow. But it is the ultimate presence. When I go to the kitchen I go through it, with much difficulty. Then it inhabits my chest. Then it becomes the first person. I mean "I." "I" follows the wind and the rain with anger. "I" knows what it means to be an Arab: proud, with no reason, humiliated, with no reason. The first person is a monkey who moved about San Francisco, Paris, Marrakesh and Bahrain. In a cage, in the bottom of a merchant boat. Also from bedroom to bedroom, but that's a later tale. A tale for insomniacs.

I am sometimes a first person and sometimes a third. My body takes over and moves like a planet on its own, in the crowded streets of an Arab town.

One day this "I" became a palm tree. I was hurting. And thirsty. I sheltered birds and spiders. I thought my immobility was a destiny with no appeal. But spring came, and I did not flower. So I understood that I was not a tree but human. It made my best friend cry.

HOUSEHOLD APPLES

Bassimeh had what seemed to be a huge river, huge for the child I was, huge also for the other child who drowned in it. We took, my father and I, the Beirut-Damascus train. A twelve hour ride for seventy miles, in order to buy apples. The train stopped at Zabadani, and kids sold paper baskets full of tiny apples. We ate them one by one until we arrived at my aunt's house in Damascus with sticky hands and flies around the mouth. We arrived drunk, rolled on the carpet, and slept under the white mosquito net. Outside, the heat, as usual, was buzzing.

CHURCH

Today a Patriarch of the Church died. Shrunk in his bed. I am not sorry. I always hated the Church because its priests hovered above my father like vultures. They wanted to have his Muslim soul, and he gave a good fight against his conversion. My Greek mother had candles above his head. She was burning olive oil to the Virgin Mary. But he was hiding in the closet in order to think of God and the forest, and recite his Koranic prayers. Then one day, when he was on his death bed, they asked him if he wanted to go to paradise. He said yes. I came close to him and told him to beware. He did not hear. They baptized him in a hurry, and then they got scared. In those days the whole city of Beirut could have been burned in a religious war. So they let his body have a Muslim funeral.

Speaking of paradise: my friend does not want to go to paradise because she dislikes blue and white and does not want to be with Jesus, wandering around with pigeons, as in Cairo Airport, dropping dirt on her head. So, we shall go to hell.

But there is a Day of Judgment. I am familiar with the Muslim one: two angels visit the grave on the day of death, one bearing a rake and the other, an iron weight. A third angel appears and begins to question the dead man. If the questions are answered to the satisfaction of the inquisitor, two more angels arrive with robes of dazzling whiteness. They lift the corpse and hold it until the Day of Judgment.

If the inquisitor angel is dissatisfied, the first two angels are recalled, the one pushing the corpse underground with the iron weight, the other proceeding to drag the body up again, this unrestful process also continuing without cessation till the Day of Judgment.

But which angels, the Christian or the Muslim ones, will accompany my father unto the presence of God?

BUSINESS

William H. Gass doesn't know it, but poets live in commercial outposts. They sell their words, then they buy back their own words, with their blood. Ever since we sold oil to some nations, the price of land in the cemeteries has gone up. Very rich people can even die twice. They can afford it.

As for me, I am afraid of my first death. It is a marriage with the unknown. It has already been dreamt by my friend Carla. Some of us used to phone each other our dreams as soon as we got up. And Carla had this dream, one night last September. "They asked me," she said, "to go and visit a cemetery in order to see how the dead are buried. I went. A woman with long black hair was sitting on a horse. She was dead and was holding against her belly a purple cushion. They were launching her horse at full speed against a forest so that, clashing with the trees, she would be reduced to ashes and disappear. But the thing was not working. So they threw the woman and her horse against the trees, and again and again nothing happened. The corpse again and again refused to die."

So I don't know how I am going to die in this city where money and death are intermingled. They sell death in Beirut as they sell wine in France. For pleasure. They beat a prisoner to death to get his shirt even though they can just take it. But they like to kill him. They call it a transaction.

My best friends go hunting. They sell the dead birds, buy cartridges, kill other birds. The woman I live with in this house is waiting for rain. I thought we could buy mineral water and sprinkle the roof. Buy the rain. Winter is lazy. There are billions of human beings on earth and billions of objects for each one of them. We calculated that each person is worth one dollar. This makes a lot of money walking in the streets, and I shall end my life with money as I started with money, my mother having paid the midwife. When I die, who is going to pay? Nobody will claim my body, but the city will mourn.

II TWENTY-FIVE YEARS LATER

PLACE
So I have sailed the seas (again), and once more came to a little town by the Bay, in California, where I hear airplanes in my sleep, and Duke Ellington, no, I'm confused, it's Kay Davis who's singing "Lush Life"; I hear flowers grow in the garden.

WEATHER
Who assigned numbers to the seasons? There's a season for love, one for hatred, and all these grey seasons that we turn over like pages, looking through their foliage as if we were inhabiting some penitentiary, under hard ceilings, with little windows and a lot of humidity. We faint and die over seasons, not unlike the bodies found lying on deserts, usually at short distance from water.

MY HOUSE
It's when I sold my parents' house that I realized all the things I could have done with it. It felt mine just after I had practically given it away. Now, my ghost wanders in it, and I try to call it back and it refuses to join me: from now on we will lead separate lives.

A PERSON
She comes at six in the morning and, at my door, throws the world. This has been happening for years and I haven't seen her yet. She must have aged. Was she young to start with?

My morning cup of coffee tastes poison: do favorable winds ever blow over the Arab East?

WIRES
There's a mountain in front of me, and I can describe all the hues of the water and the distant hills that turn pink in the summers, but anyone who deals with paradise knows that something always casts a shadow on our bliss: in my case it's the wires that cross my immediate horizon. I have to accommodate my vision, see through them . . . indeed, there are wars where one expects them the least.

THE CHURCH
Since churches, mosques or synagogues don't provide shelter for the homeless I developed a dislike for them. Students of creative writing ought to write Dante, asking him to enlarge his hell and make room for these obsolete structures.

MY HOUSE
I reside in cafés: they are my real homes. In Beirut my favorite one has been destroyed. In Paris, Café de Flore is regularly invaded by tourists . . . Yes, there's one on a northern Greek island where I go secretly. Neither the FBI nor the CIA can find that place. My mind has many houses: it's drafty in here, and noisy, angels discuss reality and virtuality while I sit, like a deposited package, at Bugatti's, not far from the ocean.

POLITICS
Since there's one world power, one president, one ideology, one politically correct line of thought, pretty soon one currency, and unisex stores, I can say that the world has reached a mystic state, the perfect achievement of monotheism.

PEOPLE
Who says that animals aren't people? I just spent a week with bears in the People's Republic of Sequoia Park. Good Lord! Have I just committed an indiscretion that will put the government's spy agencies on their tails?

VITAL DATA

Where there's life there's files: My Afghan kilim has stripes of a yellow color obtained from pomegranate dyes. The Moroccan one was made south of Meknès. It took a cherry tree to make the dining room table. My bed is in the bedroom, with linen of real cotton. On the wall I hang an American Indian Yeti rug next to a small painting by Russell Chatham. In the kitchen a toaster, red and hand-made in England, dominates the scene. Everything is presided over by the mountain.

EDUCATION

I read Flaubert's *L'Education Sentimentale* at eighteen. The young men around didn't look like Flaubert's hero and therefore didn't get the chance to become my lovers. Somebody told me once, in Mexico City, that I grew up like grass, not knowing that I wished I did.

BUSINESS

The human body is one's capital. Savage capitalism creates savage pornography. Women of color get paid less in their own countries than white slaves. All this can be easily computed, save the tears, the heartbreaks, the deterioration.

MY HOUSE, THIS PLACE AND BODY

In a house I care for the windows, only and always. Now I am seeing a mountain and in the foreground a pine tree open like an umbrella, spread against the bones and crevasses of Mount Tamalpais. The bay gets to be dark green and the boats greyish. This house doesn't seem to have any walls.

THE SAME PERSON

He had cancer recur three times but didn't expect anyone to feel sorry for him. Each time he made a will, then tore to bits the carefully written document. He recently died in a car accident. The police knocked at my door, asking questions. I never saw him, I said, lying.

WEATHER

The two things I love most are the sea and the weather. They often mix, influence each other, create strange phenomena on the Coast. The weather makes me quiver when it changes over the sea. The most interesting piece of news in the morning paper is the weather report. That's what I wanted to do a few years ago: take a VW bus across the U.S., drive in all directions with Sim and Laura Kleege and send weather reports. Oh, we did it a few times, then drove into New York in a snow storm. From Laura's 34th floor we watched the snow fall and in the process erase the city. On the white wall that ensued we wrote a few lines and then, exhausted, fell asleep. In an indeterminate hour we woke up within a gigantic white elephant.

PLACE

In one of my childhood's classrooms there were two lakes, framed and placed on the wall. (I later learned their names but it didn't matter). Thus, the first lakes I ever saw were on paper (and in a foreign country), but they left such a mark on my brain that no other surface of water, be it ocean or fountain, ever puzzled my imagination as much as they did. That was my first voyage in sight's clarity. I sailed under their winds regularly, and returned home all wet, in the late hours of my private night.

PEOPLE

In Italy I love the culture of the poor, which conceals good will and courtesy. In this small town by the Bay I don't see any lack of food, any slum, any homeless family (the latter have been carted away). But another kind of poverty is flooding, is pervasive, I mean moral poverty: the good people of Sausalito applaud and rejoice when their government bombs out of existence big chunks of Iraq and showers that country's population with depleted uranium. Their side's weapons of mass destruction are the democratic and peace-loving messengers of the New Order: missiles are the new prophets.

MY HOUSE MY CAT MY COMPANY

My mind's fire is burning little pieces of paper. I like steam, vapor, fog. I must be hiding terrible things. My cat has disappeared. In the back of the garden she had been recently chased by a rat, and as I was witnessing the scene she felt humiliated. Latifa's special plate sits near the garbage bin, covered with milk, regularly, and as regularly cleaned. Ever since that disappearance, which once in a while I call negative epiphany (given that Latifa has become a vision as intense as the Visions of Cody and that she appears under the car wheels when I drive too fast, or on the roof when it leaks), I secretly carry, tucked under my heart, a new layer of guilt that clouds my view of the mountain and cools my temperature down. We painted the house the colors of an Italian villa with the belief that this will bring Latifa back, her humiliation redeemed.

POLITICS

My stomach aches when it's hungry and distracts me from any other business: these are the politics of the belly. I also get involved in complicated situations. Last month, while the rains were pouring, some solicitor came up the stairs to sell some strange religious ideas. I ran for my gun, just in case, I thought, and due to my proverbial clumsiness, something dreadful happened, the gun was triggered and shot a bullet right into the chest of the visitor, who was thus inadvertently killed. I called, and the police arrived with helmets on (I could have sworn that they were a bunch of football players). The (unpleasant) body was carefully carried away. An inspector engaged me in a long conversation while I was getting exasperated, as my lawyer was still on his way. He started asking what I thought were benign questions.

"You are a writer of fiction," he said.

And I replied, "Nonsense, what I write is reality, what I *do* is fiction."

"But Madam," he said, "you just shot and killed a man, that's no fiction, is it?"

I replied that I didn't shoot anybody, that I had been legitimately scared and shaky, and that it was the gun, which by itself shot at a stubborn target. I added that as nobody witnessed the fact, not even my own self, everything having happened so fast, the whole thing was pure fiction, a creation of our minds, a faulty induction.

"Come on," said the inspector, his face flushing red, "you are pulling my leg!"

"I beg your pardon," I hurried, "metaphors forbidden in my vicinity." Noticing his confusion I made a proposition: "I will phone," I said, "my good friend Professor Friedman at City College, who's Director of Aristotelian Studies on Volition, Causes and Effects, and you can audit his class. It won't cost you much and will help you in your dealings with all matters of this sort."

MORE VITAL DATA

The person who was talking in the previous section has been committed to a mental institution but a good lawyer and a lot of money were able to prove that her gun had indeed accidentally released its bullet.

EDUCATION

Once in a while I go down to my garden and it's always an informing trip, although an enchantment too. One day the sage looked dry and dying and when I gave it some water it straightened up its branches, as if to thank me, and sent out a thin wave of perfume. I also remember the season when I began to dislike weeds. I furiously uprooted all kinds of tiny plants that I considered harmful, illegitimate. All I did after much labor was to make room for more resistant weeds that strangled the azaleas, marigolds and carnations . . . (small, bellicose countries, beware. Don't make it easier for super predators to swallow you up). I love my roses: they tell me that love comes with thorns, which I wish I had known sooner. But God forbid that I will go to roses for an education: I had an orange tree—whom I named La Callas: it was a living opera. Its fragrance was a song, its shade, a spot for ecstasy, its fruits, nature-blown balls of fire. A few weeks ago and for a few hours the temperature fell below zero. That was enough for my tree to catch a cold and die, as if on stage, when the music died out and the people had left.

BUSINESS

When once I asked her wherefrom the sun rose she replied angrily that that was none of my business. Later, whenever she was mad at me she would say "and now you would know where the sun comes from." That was my mother, of course, but then I did have a happy childhood . . . During my last stay in Beirut, Lebanon, it wasn't the war and the damage it did to people and things that pained me most but, rather, what people are currently doing to their own faces. The booming business in town is face lifting. Faces are being transformed at a scary pace. There's something demonic about the surgeries which give, for example, French noses to some heavily built Arab women. You would think that people are punishing themselves for the cruelty that they inflicted during the war years, although that's not what they claim. They need a change they will tell you; if it's impossible to move into a new house (or a new morality) then move away from your old appearance, remodel your ears, get rid of your wrinkles, raise your eyebrows, permanently swell your lips and spray yellow hues on your hair. It sounds like people are wearing their death masks before the hour prescribed by their fate. Yes, that's what it is, the new technology of beauty.

THAT SAME PERSON

As it was time to take care of the garden I looked for ads in the *Pacific Sun* and picked up a gardener. He arrived the next day in an old beaten-up truck and, with a broad smile. I liked him instantly. When he spoke, he betrayed a heavy accent. What's your name I asked, and he said: Alyosha. I told him that with such a name he should among other things be able to revivify my orange tree. I must say that he tried and must say that he failed. We had at least some political discussion, my favorite kind of talk.
"You left Russia," I said. "Why?"
"I listened, as a child, to Voice of America."
"Why?" I insisted.

"For the music. Savage music. Trumpets and trombones."

"The trumpets and the trombones led you all the way to California?"

"I grew up in Vladivostock, not too far from Alaska."

"Why didn't you go instead to Moscow?"

"No ocean in Moscow. Big empty spaces but no ocean."

"My garden doesn't overlook the ocean."

"Your garden is nice, like grandma's garden in Vladivostock."

"Hmm . . . do you plan to return there someday?"

"No. I love the United States. Good government."

"Alyosha, you're full of illusions. . . ."

"Governments that have their capital cities near water are good governments. You see, Washington is near the Atlantic. It's open, open. I'm going to visit it one day."

I thought to myself: no two waves are alike.

WIRES

It was in the movies that I saw barbed wires for the first time. "Movietone" comes to mind: the show always opened with world news, and World War II was in full swing, sending to Beirut's cinemas luminous black-and-white images from the war zones. This way I followed Spitfires and Stukas falling like birds onscreen, looked at the English fleet cut waves and saw all kinds of human beings press themselves against fences made of wire: old people, women with sad looks, children with faces that could have been my own. When years later I came to California and found myself driving constantly by beautiful but fenced ranches I reacted with anguish, unable to shake off the war associated with these deadly lines of twisted metal, when at the cataclysm's end everybody and everything looked alike, the displaced, the survivors of the camps, victims and conquerors, civilians and soldiers . . . a flood of misery broken loose.

But then, at unexpected moments, when the mind is free of associations, when one's gaze runs into some electric lines on which birds take a rest, or wires become clotheslines, or simply drawings; they can be writings.

WEATHER

Spring remains deadly, like red roses. Starting on the second solstice of the year it makes vegetation sprout and our shoulders grow wings. We fly high above orchards, buzz around mountain peaks, spawn, leave nests, engage in fist fights, seek former passions, go out to sea. In Delphi spring smells of sage; the olive fields sway their silver-green masses. We come close to the resurrection of the old myths. Elsewhere in the Mediterranean bushes turn pugnacious, poppies bleed, cyclamens compete with butterflies in catching the light. It's the time when the weather envelops us like a warm bath. There are other weathers too. A snow storm has eaten up travelers on the North Plains and thrown cowboys and cows into the core of the fury. They were carried miles away from their barns and fell, heavy and dead. Weather is matter's pure volition. One can experience ecstasy on February days over the Bay Bridge: the air is crisp and makes us weightless. It suspends our thoughts and we become pure life. We are sponges and absorb the weather, our habitat. When some shadow glides under the sun it glides over our eyes too. Fog privileges memory and rains alter our sense of time.

PLACE

I was central and became peripheral. My feet were adapted to the ground. While swimming, circles of water originated from my body. Whoever I didn't know didn't exist . . . I carried my own space and fearlessly looked out. Then, what happened? It happened that I gradually *learned* that my bed belonged to my mother, she had bought it, that a rubber ball didn't bounce once I drew the scissors into it; I saw my doll lose its hair, heard the nun at school tell a lie; then at age nine or ten Helen, my friend, changed schools, and I didn't own her presence any more. . . it will take another life to tell it all. So what did I do? I moved from city to city, travelled from person to person, and then I tried to define myself through writing, but that doesn't work, no, not at all, it adds fiction to the fiction I became, and from that place where I had a sense of my absolute importance I reached a fogged

Olympus from which the gods and goddesses had long departed: I'm in a disorienting wilderness.

PEOPLE

They used to want revolution, the poor and the rich, but that meant different things, I concede; nevertheless it was desired by all. In my Beirut days we used to meet endlessly in cafés full of infiltrators, but we didn't care, we talked loud for all to listen. We were foolish and paid for it dearly. People were being assassinated as if they were flies and we went on dreaming, thinking that each defeat would lead to victory. Then, suddenly, the whole world was deflated. Flat on its face. We sang with Cheikh Imam, "Guevara died, Guevara died." Funeral lines were multiplying. We followed them. We thought that we had to go through the tunnel of death to start living again. Beautiful houses fell, most of them collapsed upon whole families sitting at dinner. Every community seemed to want out. Every child wanted a Disneyland. Children were being burned with fire hoses in Vietnam. We thought that one day they would lead happy lives, meaning the few who would survive. Hope, like wild-fire, was being fanned by the winds of war. One day we noticed that the price for bananas at the point of origin was not going up but rather crumbling. It was the same story everywhere, refugees waiting under their tents, political prisoners dying in hunger strikes. While revolutionary hopes were receding prosperity in the Western world was rising . . . people were perplexed. Evil was not being punished by God. Some former revolutionaries managed to join the party of the rich. They visited the South Seas, bought houses, played the piano. They succeeded without the revolution and concluded that any form of thought was superfluous for the well-being of mankind. Even the notion of mankind became suspicious.

Almost everything I see is useless: but people want more, of anything . . . very few (myself included) give much to lost causes. When they recycle their old bottles they feel generous enough. They are impervious to such a debate.

(30)

Years ago, people who were totally unsettled appeared to me as remote as mountains. It was hard to figure out who they were and what they were living for. I myself didn't answer these questions but I had a strange sense of freedom, of not being quite human, feeling at ease, or rather identifying with drafts of air, dispersing dry leaves and balloons, taking taxis just because they were staring at me, sometimes following strangers and then protecting myself with my arms, with the type of innocence one doesn't even know that one has.

People looked friendly then, through my heart's surrounding haze, through their inexistence. That empty space that I was carrying within me was my protection while I had no money to count on. How I managed then to go to jazz concerts I don't know. I would stand by the door a long time and suddenly go in and sit and listen. I loved to have my fingers around the chilled glasses of the few drinks I was sipping. And the sounds! Paradise had been of an easy access. If Thelonius Monk played for you for a couple of dollars wouldn't you have thought that you were with the right people at the right time?

HOUSE, MY BREATH AND WINDOW

Hotels are the structures of our dreams. I prefer them to houses. When I pass in front of one, let's say, in Italy, my heart beats and I wonder if my life shouldn't have been totally alien to the one I lived. San Francisco's hotels appeal to my imagination most: not the big palaces, no, for they are mausoleums. But the little, hard-to-find, hidden, rather messy and shoddy ones that shelter the desperadoes of this whole continent, are poetic verses made of slime, death-wishes, of defeats; yet, they have a strange vibrancy that is hypnotic. I will catch fevers in there, hear neighborhood music, behave like man or woman, at that point nothing will matter save the need to add to one's life a day at a time, until, until what, until the horizon implodes. The hotel rooms, small and often with chipped or broken windows, bring me closer to the weather on speaking terms with the fog.

POLITICS

From the iron tables of the State Department divine fire is thrust on Baghdad and destruction is willed of the ancestral laws of Hammurabi. History continues on its path, circular, spherical, orbiting the mind like earth around the sun. You can go as far as to Sydney, Australia, the sky will be different but the terror the same. We're starting the end of a year, a century, millennium: what an alignment of planets! The politics of the heart are more complicated; they're put on back burners, they're explosive. We ignore them as much as we can but they haunt and sear us with an equally deadly fire.

From the ashes of the physical heart memories rise with a life of their own and that's what people call "voices." From Madrid to Beirut, whichever road you take, North or South, you will encounter young girls who cry, heads hidden in their arms at café tables, because their fathers chased their lovers away. Individual little rebellions are crushed in this kind of low-intensity warfare.

FINAL VITAL DATA

We are strangers to ourselves, that's a given; then why do we sign our letters or our legal documents, why do we carry cards and use fixed numbers of identity? We are playing games, games that involve pictures and money. Any map carefully scanned tells us that there is no uncharted piece of land, nowhere to escape to and start an anonymous life. We go inward, of course, but there one feels that the "outside" world is contagious, inner and outer realms porous and often indistinguishable, if not interchangeable . . . These old problems are becoming obsolete: the subject, the object . . . all this is nonsense. I wonder what tigers think of us: clumsy, cluttered with clothes, paralyzed with fear? Pitiful beings, that's what we are; but then we went to the moon, didn't we, we overtook angels in their flights, we're measuring the universe, and then, here comes circularity; with measurement we bring death to what we measure.

Childhood's sun is forever young, ball of fire giving substance to anything it touches. Then the knowledge that we are dealing with just an overpowered nuclear reactor follows and depression seeps into our bones . . . if the sun itself will disappear what are we doing with all these museums, archives, stored films, all the data piling in the sanctuaries of future oblivion? Still, if we didn't have delusions we wouldn't have gone to cabarets and given it all for a glass of beer, in these rare moments when we did everything right.

I still love the moon. The hell with the fact that she will disappear. I saw her the other night sitting on Angel Island, her face wide open, watching the view and breathing the weather. Japanese herring boats were busy depleting the seawaters and I couldn't care less because the moon was there, close-by, as happy as I was, as bewildered by so much beauty, her own, I mean. She is an old-time friend, a veteran of our conversations, so familiar that she tames the world, makes it home.

EDUCATION
At moments I feel that planet Earth's whole mass is my own, that we're one and the same. Air is ours too, to whom else would it belong? And the Day of Judgment will be ours, when the mind will see the other side of its own reality. Nature is all around, in the harbor's boats as well as in Death Valley, in electrical bulbs, plants and worms. But Nature also goes *through* us, fills us, moves through us like radiation; is probably an enormous mass of radiations with different densities, encompassing infinity, and there's infinity to Nature's own definition, an inner infinity that reduces it, in the frame of our logic, to nothingness. We can follow it neither in its immensity nor in its evanescence. What are we thinking about, then?

Thinking wouldn't function without memory, for even the present is memory aware of itself. We want our memories to join the world, be objects to which we can return at will, and not what they are, electronic images, ephemeral waves, uncertain visitations from the past, ever-new creations of our brain.

That's probably why (as a species) we invented writing: to gratify ourselves with the illusion—and the comfort—that certain things, certain mental operations will be arrested in their becoming and turned into stored, refrigerated materials. This can also explain why any written page looks like a grid, the side of a cage, a screen: lines easily become wires, barbed wires keeping thoughts from overflowing, keeping inmates from escaping.

But reality escapes.

Writing opened a new line in the flesh of Being; it's not only a tool but a mode of apprehension of reality. It "uncovered" a new sense (added to touch, hearing . . .); writing was not enslaved by the written. The first act of writing was a mutation.

Mind works in introspection, works like cinema, filming itself and projecting (simultaneously) the results on its own inner walls. It constantly pushes (tries) these boundaries, limits, which resemble the invisible and virtual lines that separate water currents within the ocean, air drafts within air, boundaries both flexible and tenacious.

We are dealing with a veritable passion play. Writing, (*écriture*), necessitated since its inception a whole field of experimentation with language, languages, poetics, which help the mind in its push against its own elastic limits, when it puts these limits under examination, under stress, discovering in that ongoing process its own open-ended, unstable definition.

ANOTHER PERSON
At the war's beginning he was still handsome. He formed a militia and distributed roles, rifles, special assignments. Some of his men hit their targets, others died, flat on the

ground, their arms open. He, my friend, went on killing, and "liberating" until all sides were defeated. He returned home, two fingers missing, living alone, not having had the time to get married, a crucifix over his bed, a tiny kitchen behind his living room. His dying room.

THE FIRST PERSON

Can a woman remember any first occurrence? It's always so oceanic. It all hangs together. Where's the first cat, where its kittens? My first slippers? The little boy who kissed me goodnight when he was a guest (and an orphan), where, or who is he now? I'm not even sure of his name.

There was a guy, in Beirut, who was smoking cigarettes behind my half-opened shutters, the myrtle berries' smell coming in with the breeze, and the lamp projecting his shadow on the little alley's stone wall. Why hadn't he ever spoken to me? We must have been scared of each other . . .

And there was a stranger who was regularly coming home. When had it started? I wasn't in school yet. I disliked him intensely. My mother asked me to call him "uncle" but I refused and wouldn't change my mind. One day, I remember that clearly, sharply, this non-uncle arrived in a huge and shiny car all chrome and glass and brilliant black doors and our house filled with excitement and I spent time by the window looking at that engine, and at the end of his visit he asked my parents if he could give me a ride along the Corniche and they said yes and he drove what I learned later was one of the first Buicks in town, drove it by the sea, the Corniche was then planted with palm trees and smelled algae and salt, and I felt grownup and we returned home and he sat me on his knees and said: "And now, will you call me 'uncle?'" And I said, "No!"

HOUSEHOLD APPLES

I'm also sure that there are some rotting, now, in the kitchen. Apples are not ordinary fruits. They grow in every mythology. One can play billiards with those that are round, deep-red and shiny. They roll on Cezanne's napkins. Are they edible? As a child I went through baskets and baskets in a garden by the river, in Bassimeh and the valley that leads to Damascus. One bite and the apple was thrown away and a new one was bitten, this endlessly. I would sleep with their smell all over me, use them like stones to keep the goat away, the goat we ended up eating come September. These apples were tiny and loaded with fragrance. They had a name, like people, they were called Zabadanis. I used to rub them on my face to transfer some of their redness, and string them along the railway tracks A good half a century later I planted an apple tree in my Sausalito garden. It doesn't like the fog but it's living all right. A few blossoms, a few apples a year, we understand each other.

CHURCH

My quarrel with the Church is so ancient that I often think that I lived in Spain once, under the Inquisition. But once in a while I enter a Greek church and hear my mother's voice mingled with other voices and noises . . . I look at the Greek Virgin, always with a child, always staring and wondering, and I somehow relate to her. I pay her a visit, I tell her stay where you are, don't go into the mess outside, you don't need to, and her wide and wild eyes give me reassurance.

BUSINESS

Some people, probably most, die many times . . . not each time for a better life. They carry a halo, which is the remembrance made visible of the dark zones they have entered, the crossing over, that surrender.

I am still after a weather that will make me feel renewed, a tormented landscape whose winds will bring me their stories. London tempts me as a place for fun and adventure but when I'm there I think of Italy with its small towns, its illuminated and frescoed churches, its secrets. She comes close to some ideal but it won't do for long. I turn to the Syrian desert for sheer enchantment but run into trucks. I came close, once, to Afghanistan but stopped at its western frontier. I took a plane just to fly over Macchu Picchu and went altogether out of Time, leaving my soul—and its memories—behind. The night sky followed. Back on Earth I was a person nobody knew. Beds, rugs, forks and knives, anything you can barter or sell is superfluous . . . The business of life is about not being where you are.

III FURTHER ON

PLACE

As for oceans, I sailed a few, then flew over, over my own story, to a little town in Mexico where a sailor was particularly good looking, and discovered a bar and there met a woman caught between two people, a foreigner who was drinking too much and a young girl, both attracted to her and to the soft wind, outside, with the sound of the ocean touching the beach.

WEATHER

There are days when the storm refuses to break out and in those days pains are born within my limbs and behave like spirits with a will of their own, leaving me helpless against this invasion. Once, I was crossing a garden, a huge one planted with tulips whose color was red-wine, dispersed among iridescent blue flowers with leaves still retaining the dew. I thought: on such a day, a person from history to whom I'm particularly attached looked at this space and welcomed this kind of weather. She was a queen exiled in France amid brutal surroundings. She was banished, later, and died in Cologne.

MY HOUSE

Often I buy books about houses and start, page after page, to move into different apartments or dwellings that make one wonder if glass walls separate us from nature or if they are meant to make us feel at one with the trees. My favorite trees around houses, cabins, shacks are oaks.

A PERSON

People are here to betray. There's a person who loved me to death, not to my death or hers, but to the death of a person I loved. So, when she aged, my resentment made me speechless. I let her guess why I was angry, and that was punishment enough. I wonder who invented the ugly word "punishment"; it was probably God who established the word, and the deed.

WIRES

A straight line, I was taught, was good for hanging clothes, but I saw wires that were crooked and used for crowns of thorns. I also saw a cage with wires that were intended to protect a canary from predators, the cat and the dog. One morning I found the bird dead from lack of water. I had the night before watered the garden, thoroughly, but had forgotten to fill the little can with the precious water it demanded.

THE CHURCHES

On Sunday bells toll and women in black are swallowed by a white structure that I never enter. These creatures come out of the church with the same expression on their faces that they had previously and they smell of incense and wax. That's how it is, on this island, and elsewhere.

MY HOUSE

Hotel rooms hold a fascination: there's a sense of loneliness that I sometimes experienced in them that still does haunt me. How did I survive that feeling of void, or rootlessness, or uselessness that possessed me more than a few times in cities such as Paris and New York? How did I climb that wall of nothingness to attain a perspective from which a next day was possible? But houses can be much worse, they can be pierced baskets from which one's life oozes and drains into the gutters. I discovered, by chance, in a book, that Thoreau's attention was transfixed by permanent structures. The forest, the boat, the fresh air were not enough to give him serenity . . . he was constantly looking for a house!

POLITICS
Television works differently from cocaine: it dumbs the spirit and creates a kinship with cartoons. Children have grown tails and are asking to perform in Disneyland and parents hurry to agree. Soon, governments (I mean the few that will remain) will have no trouble running a depleted planet.

PEOPLE
Sound research has proved that people pollute the world and, as they're part of it, pollute themselves. . . . Immaterial people probably exist on other planets, and we're eager to get in touch with them. They won't need olives, bread, or a Mercedes sport car . . . and I doubt that our ideas will be of any interest to them . . . they may have better ones, or none at all. Who knows?

VITAL DATA
I have established a sound relation with the universe. Of that, I'm sure. I move freely between the sun and the moon, I go further, I plunge into black holes and emerge intact. I ride on comets, count galaxies. I'm on speaking terms with light-years, all this since I traveled in a matter of seconds to the Universe's edge and suspected that the strange movement that I witnessed, once there, was the beginning of an abyss.

EDUCATION
I think about water, often: I can't hold it in my hands for any length of time, cut it with a knife or understand why it runs with such a happiness. We think that something is certain, but then a little screw is missing, nothing works, the mind remains bewildered. Still, when I *love* water, I have no problem coming close to its being.

BUSINESS
Those who make in no time billions of dollars stop eating, drinking, fucking, buying flowers . . . they spend time dreaming of more money.

Some don't dream, they kill. I met people of that sort in a restaurant in the fifteenth arrondissement of Paris. One night I was in that special place with good food, and there was a table with three beautiful women and a man whom I recognized, having seen him in newspapers quite often. His hair was glued to his temples, he had make-up on his cheeks. . . . He was speaking in the accent of one of the North-African countries I know, and exuding much venom. Against one of the walls of the restaurant was a table occupied by "people-watchers," and they were at front-row and showing it by being loud. Their pleasure was sickening. To the left of the entrance I noticed three guys, three thugs. They had a mountain of food under their noses and were conspicuously enjoying their dinner. Something stirred in my stomach. They were bodyguards, obviously, and certainly armed. This was not a hunting place, but it had all the elements of the leftovers of a hunt.

MY HOUSE, THIS PLACE, MY BODY
The sun shines through my windows with no difficulty as they are wide open. I try to touch the light but it disappears at that very moment; all I do is make shadows with my fingers. Then I think that the world is somewhere else, in Mexico, in India. . . Why should it always be in a named place? Why should it, altogether, *be*?

THE SAME PERSON
Am I my body, and/or my soul, and does an angel define us otherwise? But when I carry pain whenever I'm awake and wherever I go, the question becomes serious. An acute awareness of oneself is not always a blessing.

WEATHER
It's always back to my favorite thing: the weather. Since childhood, I've listened to thunder because it is awesomeness itself. I also always loved soft rains, their sexual appeal with no sex involved . . . no jealous lover can ever suspect the competition they represent. When one cloud passes over another, I tremble and when a patch of blue pierces a grey sky I soar like an angelic figure.

(42)

Some rains are deadly: they announce an apocalyptic melt-down, the cosmic ocean's self-destruction. They make us lose all points of reference by creating pools in which all specifications drown. They push us back to our abstractions and in that dismal state of affairs we err in cities, carrying the knowledge of that disaster as baggage. Hotel clerks get suspicious and refuse to give us a key. We wander for a while in some train station and when we have a change of mind we re-enter the city and spend the night walking.

But what about the inner tempests where high seas of anger unleash their fury against the mind? Mind and stomach merge in those times, fuse into deadly rays, probe the inner soul as no hurricane can do to the Atlantic coasts. These inner lands sometimes take the shape of real territories, Syria, Lebanon, California . . . where we live inside and outside the self, not distinguishing a missile hitting a house from some devastating thought. The onslaught of History on the brain creates storms that batter the imagination with more destructive power than any cataclysmic weather. Some of us are familiar with these private disasters which accumulate and become daily bread and daily experience.

PLACE
One apple is sitting in a blue bowl of stoneware made by Eileen Curtis. Every surrounding thing moves away from a collection of objects which were attracted to a square shelf. Do they feel at last secure in that setting or are they, for their misfortune, and rather like me, unable to rest? They form a beautiful unit that only painters can appreciate, giving the rest of their lives to reproduce, sometime, somewhere, with any material at hand, the ecstasy of the apple and of the bowl.

PEOPLE
I particularly love Fra Angelico, Angelico while painting angels. He does not paint them, he creates angels who have thus escaped God's creation. He sprays gold on their hair and around them. Each time I went to visit him, he was

absent, out of Florence, not yet in Sienna, on his way to Arezzo, just back from Padua but not yet at home. . . . I rest my hand on one of his painted walls and feel his angel's flesh, the one who forever announces the coming of a baby. People like Angelico do not come in number.

MY HOUSE MY CAT MY COMPANY

Let me have the courage to say that all three belonged to my mother, because that's true, a reality that has shaped my health and desires. Her cat, named Bijou (as I have already said), slept in her mosquito net. She loved that weight hanging over her sleep. Bijou had a huge house for her promenades: arched windows for watching mice in the garden, armchairs covered with damascene velvet for her claws, a kitchen stove to warm her bones. I didn't live in that house, with that cat, or in my mother's company, I just crossed all these entities like a draft of air.

POLITICS

Dimensions have swelled and industries spit columns of smoke and hatred. Hating has become a passion so intense that it is burning us with it. We dress our enemies with silk and cotton, manufacture shoes for their feet, feed them chestnut paste, burn incense on their altars, provide salutations, write music for their ears . . . and then, then . . . we are either eaten by them or we lose interest.

MORE VITAL DATA

The U.S. government is gathering vital information about all the country's dogs. Because citizens are already being over-processed, many computers are idle and many people out of jobs. The good government of the people, by the people, and for the people, has decided to become a caring institution for animals, too. It is starting with dogs. Much research is done on the laws of classification for these particular creatures. There will be problems with spots and food habits, but they will be solved as they arise. Cats are waiting for their turn with the kind of apprehension that Third World populations used to have when they saw coming toward them the first cameras and tapes carried by strangers. Doctors are keeping track of viruses and poets of rabbits. There's nothing to worry about. All this will make death look merciful.

EDUCATION
One day I gave an orange to a monkey and what did he do with it? He ate it. I was surprised. I expected him to play with it, smell or squeeze it, thank me for it . . . I don't know. Somehow, I was disappointed. I realized that we humans are trained like singing dogs, tamed like dying lions, programmed to think and hesitate. My monkey took the orange and, in a moment of perfect intelligence, he ate it.

BUSINESS
If the business of life is happiness I will describe for you my linen sheet: it's soft and cool, and flexible. I will say it's friendly. Friendly to me, and to whomever visits. Then I will look at a wall, a wall in the desert. You will call it a ruin and I will disagree and the dispute will shatter our pleasure. In Cash Creek, California, the river is young and capricious. It talks to the sky, envelops young girls with its curls, arouses young men with its smoothness. There, in Yosemite, the deer rest a knowing eye on the ferns. The snow is a protective blanket, until the sun comes out again and is amazed by all that white beauty. But in some places, like Nebraska, people burn their clothing out of boredom. They haven't moved far enough West.

THAT SAME PERSON
His name was Charles, and he disliked his name. He called himself Peter. Peter? Petering? Saint Peter's? It was his uncle who had named him Charles, after his own grandfather. Unsure of the fitness of the name, Peter took another one: Vassili. When people started addressing him in Greek he felt embarrassed; he couldn't go to Russia for a similar reason. He also thought that the United States was big enough in which to disappear. . . . As he loved Beethoven, he re-christened himself Ludwig, with some pride.

(45)

But it turned out that his neighbor, who had grown up in East Germany, was originally called Ludwig, but on natural-ization day, had chosen Charles for his new, American, self. The postman confused the two Charleses. Charles the first, who kept getting mail in his old name, grew paranoid: he feared losing his girlfriend to this other Charles, who, he thought, was responsible for the problem. . . . He went back to calling himself Vassili. Now, thinking he was a Russian immigrant, nobody talked to him. As a good Catholic he went to St. Peter's Church in Santa Monica, where he had moved a while ago. The ocean was beautiful in his neigh-borhood, with its blue lines and white hair. Somehow, though, everything was upside down in his life. His anger and his confusion caused him to lose his job at the garage where he had been a specialist in brakes and transmissions. Eventually, like many other people on that particular day, he died. A cousin paid for a tomb. They had to inscribe his name on the marble headstone, and there were many family discussions over the phone. So, to find peace, they decided to inscribe on the grave marker: "Here lies Ludwig Vassili Peter Charles Gregory-Smith." The Gregory-Smiths had come from Uptown, Delaware. Our man was the only one of that name who had ever reached California.

WIRES
On television, the model of DNA looks like a simple design made of two copper wires, twisted gracefully. Could it be that Shakespeare rose out of such a configuration of elec-trons? And what about Egypt? Do countries rise from hid-den forms, and can it be that, when the forms are twisted wrongly, there are wars, massacres, collective hallucina-tions? We will find out. Everything will be found out, explained and discarded. I wish that the breeze, the warm and low desert wind, the sand dunes with ripples remain, with the sun very low, either at dawn or at dusk.

WEATHER
Every time the year makes a full turn, it's April, squeezed between two interesting months. Sausalito's weather, in

April, is indecisive: the ocean gets to be fluorescent in a maddening way, and the mountain remains green, bottle-green, a color in which there's a memory of yellow. The weather is not dramatic. It's rather tuned to the American sense of comfort. It is not balmy, not yet: never in April. It is a month that slides through our fingers.

But in Greece, it's something else. Everything in Greece happens outside the rest of the world, probably because it's there that Christ is resurrected for real. And he brings back with him an ecstasy of marine colors, of silvery clouds, fragrances from the days of the gods, and a lot of candles for the fingers of unsuspecting children.

PLACE

When we don't know simple things, such as why flowers grow secretly, we divert our attention to beaches. Then, having exhausted the possibilities of these flat surfaces—not so flat, not so bumpy—our mind wavers, floats over undefined terrains and, most often not landing anywhere, returns to its seat and habitat just to discover that new ideas are waiting for their turn to take off.

I go often to Rodeo Beach (which for decades I called Cronkite Beach), watch the little ducks and leave them to their destiny, and listen to the ocean. Oceans are the kind of place I would inhabit (but if I had been a whale it must have been light-years ago), so I stand, sometimes hurting, and face the waves. The wind plays its games with the pelicans, and the redwing black birds sound their little trumpets. They greet each other with an effervescence that enchants the hour. But nowhere as by an ocean does Time speed by. Everything is in constant, visible change. There's more than color to such an environment: there is our desire to embrace the emptiness that shelters all these events. But that "emptiness" is immense. So we lie on the beach, talk to it, kiss it . . . grains of sand try to find their way into our mouths. We spit them out.

PEOPLE

A visitor to Sausalito may very well be impressed by a billboard with a big eye on it, informing him that he just crossed into a nuclear-free zone. Would that quiet his fears? Does it mean that, if and when the Golden Gate Bridge is reduced to a memory, fallout will stay away from our hills? A few Unitarian ladies whom I know pretty well believe in the power of the will. They're luckier than I am. In the meantime the police are chasing rabbits away from gardens, because the cops consider them a serious traffic hazard. In general, the police are rather decent. In the few decades I've lived in this town, they have killed but one person: they chased a young man out of the Seven-Eleven store and shot him down. He was holding in his hand a chocolate bar that he had just purchased.

Oh yes! That very same institution that protects the (smug) residents of Sausalito harasses the most interesting man I know in the area: my friend Ross, who lives a few streets down the hill from my house and to the north. He's a veteran of the Korean War from which he returned broken, in fact shattered. A woman took him in, turned him into a craftsman, like herself, and together they made local history. Their big shack became the rallying point for many painters and a few stray writers. There was pride in being there.

That place has retained its magic although inhabited by an absence. Eileen died twenty-five years ago. The same friends still come to see Ross, sit around the same table, and think of her. We go there to bring Eileen to life in our imagination. I can watch Ross stir up big logs in the formidable iron stove. What I really see is Eileen's gaze when he was doing exactly that, when he was building a fire not only in the stove but in her body and her mind.

He's still somewhat like a vulnerable Hemingway, an old leftist with guns in one of the cupboards, a pacifist who would kick, as he repeats, the teeth out of America's military. While he's probably the last old adolescent speaking from the sixties, he *does* invest some money in mutual funds to make sure that his dwelling will not go without repairs. A craftsman he remains, but Eileen's unfired last pots and plates keep gathering dust. He continues to make his own ceramic vases, and sculptures inspired by China, making the old Chinese surfaces of smoothened Buddhas . . . but he remains best at growing salads, onions, raising a few chickens in his lush garden. When Eileen was around, he used to paint on her pots frolicking baby elephants, long-eared rabbits, or deer. She used to look at his incredibly blue eyes and hear his Lincoln, Kansas, stories. . . . The one he repeats most often is how, at eleven or twelve, he accompanied his grandpa in the robbery of a grave; how grandpa, like a skilled dentist, pulled a gold-covered tooth out of a dead man's mouth. When he pronounces the mythic word "Kansas" he stands with legs apart and torso slightly forward, as if to say that that's where America's center of gravity is to be found.

Ross drinks and laughs, and people around him become alcoholics; but as they have already lived a long life, who can blame them? Russell Chatham, indeed, of his generation the greatest painter of the West, a champion of fly-fishing and of writing about fly-fishing, used to come and sit at that rectangular table, which wine has stained and thinned down the years, and serve up his own catch of salmon with a laughter echoing Ross's. Eileen's blue stoneware pots are always filled with the garden's apples and pears, a few lemons hiding among them: Russell has some in Montana; Bill and Sally took theirs to Somocolonia, in Tuscany; Tom regularly eats his corn flakes in them, and Arden as regularly fears breaking one. Mine are in this house, which faces the mountain; they are in a closet and in my memory, where they live with Eileen, who made them; and Ross, in Portugal this summer, drinking, sometimes falling, has been working for the last three years on a sculpture representing Vasco da Gama, which he wants to offer to the little town by the Atlantic where he makes his alternate home, now that he doesn't go to Morelia, Mexico anymore, because, as he says a few times a year, that's the place where Eileen took him for their wedding.

HOUSE, MY BREATH AND WINDOW

Houses are made of windows held standing by walls. All kinds of things enter not through doors but through windows wide open on a clear sky. That's the way Gabriel came in to scare the Virgin. It was not, though, on a Halloween night . . . Jesus was born, and not yet born, and Mary was confused. Fra Angelico lived next to windows, celestial ones. He framed them with gold and took the walls away. He left shimmering lights with patches of pure red. Balls of fire and crowns made of diamonds bring their own light to his paintings; that is, if we can call the apparitions that he makes visible, "works of art." They are not due to artifice but to secret forces of nature, those we seldom deal with. His angels play trumpets while we think that we are listening to Pergolesi. These trumpets are angelic toys. Their sound comes through my window and becomes a breeze on my face when I lie, in spring, in some room away from my usual home and hometown. To one's innocence Fra Angelico brings his breath and gently puts out the candles. Then, the sun shines with restrained benevolence.

POLITICS

On Sundays, there are no government meetings, no declarations of war, and, in some cities, no buses.

FINAL VITAL DATA

As we are products of a family, we feel compelled to talk about it in order to define ourselves. It's just a habit. That's probably why I watch, intensely, movies about animals. The animals I like to watch are usually monkeys, tigers, lions, elephants, whales and dolphins. Each of these has characteristics I would have loved to have. They represent the possibilities of Being distributed among the whole animal species. But on a day I will never forget I saw on my television chimpanzees climb trees and jump from branches to branches. The particular light of the moment in which they had been filmed imparted a sense of unreality. It was as if acting were involved . . . and I started thinking that soon, when human behavior will be responsible for the disappearance of most of the animals that live on earth, "scientists" or "artists" will replace them with virtual animals, so that we will have holograms of lions in the zoos, three-dimensional elephants in the movies, with dangers included, rubber whales in museums and dolphin-like illusions performing in the sea. I shivered, suffered an incredible bout of anguish, felt bitterness on my tongue and weight in my limbs. I have the firm belief—and that contributes to my chronic insomnia—that it's already late if we want to avoid the disasters that we are preparing for ourselves.

EDUCATION
Why is there sadness in the idea of education? We are creating new coercive dogmas and new idols. But, some would say, there are the poets! Yes, there are the poets and there are the readers, and the dreamers, and the lovers . . . and they constitute the new continents to be discovered.

ANOTHER PERSON
He was chaotic: he used to forget his name and tell people he was a baron; and when they wanted to know from which estate he came, he would answer, in his Greek accent, that he was German. He would embark on a winding description of the Rhine's southern trajectory and then forget the names of the cities the river was supposed to cross. He did, once, convincingly, explain why his Greek island was green in all seasons. We did see pictures of his mother and two sisters, but as nothing was written on the back of the photographs, we had no reason either to believe him or dismiss everything he said. His hair was never combed. My impression was that he always slept on his left side, because of so many things. . . . He was not cross-eyed, no, but his eyes were each looking at a different distance. They gave a dreamy look to his face which endeared him to women. He loved women, he used to say, but he spent his days with young men, playing billiards in Alexandria. At least, that's what he

told me. When I tried to speak Greek with him he answered that he didn't understand the language, and when I showed surprise he laughed, beautifully, and said that he had had a nanny from Smyrna who had given him her own accent when he was a child, and that the accent had never left him. His English was Shakespearean and his French from Marseilles and Nice. We saw him spend money but he never invited any of us to dinner.

THE FIRST PERSON
You could see her from any street, through different angles, and then let yourself go to your dreams. They used to come from afar just to spend a few hours with her. In non-air-conditioned cafés, I spent hours looking at her through the windows, contemplating her beauty which belonged to a realm of being all her own. In the summers I would go down a winding street and then reach her and, taking off my clothes in a tall and narrow cabin, would enter her and swim.

HOUSEHOLD APPLES
I find apples in the market of any city that I visit. I find them also in contemporary paintings, or notice their ominous presence in Renaissance murals and tapestries. . . . Who chose that round and fragrant fruit to signify sin? It's unforgivable. Some sadistic person must have decided to spoil our pleasure, forever, for an apple tree is the king of trees. Apples hang like little green worlds and, sometimes, when we come too close, they blush. In the spring, their costume of flowers replaces, advantageously, the melting snow. My familiarity with them started in the hidden paradise that the Barada Valley used to be, west of Damascus. Nobody will ever find it, not even on a map, for the little village of Bassimeh had a few houses made of bricks, with dusty floors; and there was almost no visibility, even during the day, for the valley's bed is made of the river and is a torrent in winter, a dry bed in summers. . . . The children used little stones for toys, and they hit each other with those tiny weapons until a "grown-up" would show up and stop the games. My uncle owned a piece of land which was either flooded or dying of thirst, and

he felt happier there than anywhere else in the world. So did I. In a corner of that land covered with the river's sound, there were a few apple trees that he called an orchard. And that place was my own paradise.

CHURCH

There's a church that isn't a church, with paintings that aren't paintings, and, if I hadn't found my paradise already as a child, I would consider that church to be a place of ultimate ecstasy. I discovered it at random. From the railway station I was heading for Padua; the baggage felt heavy and the hour nondescript, so I entered a church I had just noticed, just to kill time. It was Giotto's chapel. Instead of being "killed," Time was resurrected as a sacred visual poem, as I entered that blue heaven with its buzzing angels and its imminent Day of Judgment. My Day of Judgment had arrived in that Chapel of the Scrovegni and I was saved.

BUSINESS

When would some anarchy ever erupt in this chartered, measured, and parceled world where living has become theater? Of course, there's misery, plenty of it, in countries of the southern latitudes, with ways unacceptable to Paris, barely tolerated in London, nonexistent in Mexico. . . . But misery does not create creative chaos; on the contrary, it dreams of order, rows of bread, straight lines of water, well-defined bank accounts.

I will need the primeval chaos that spat out stones in the Mediterranean or gave such an energy to the Indians of the Americas that they ran from the Pacific Coast to the Atlantic as if they were on an extended promenade. To think, think, and why? My friend Bob knows only what his owl tells him, and Joanne Kyger discovers every morning the existence of a world devoid of questions.

IV AT BOTH ENDS

"Love is an unfinished form of history"
—Lyn Hejinian

When in the vast eastern Syrian desert I found a mirror, I picked it up and read in it Lawrence's face; then the sky passed over, followed by a hot light. This blinded me for a while, then with my car I found my way back to the Palmyra Hotel and asked to be allowed to sleep for as long as I could. When I awoke I recited over and over again the opening poem of *The Seven Pillars*. In a state of intense passionate grief Lawrence wrote the poem, in lieu of dedication, for his young Arab lover for whom he endeavored "to liberate the Arab East," but the dream as well as the reality died right there and then. As he stated it, the young body was already eaten by worms when he entered Damascus and he had his own tears to drink for that dark victory; the tragic farce his life had become ended a decade or so later with his motorcycle's skid on a dirt road. Arabia's sands cover stacks of dreams and count forgotten passions.

One doesn't adopt the ways of the desert with impunity: the sun, for one, and other creatures, won't let you be in peace; only the stars, at night, will keep you company; but these cold beings, closer to diamonds than to lovers, will inflame your imagination into fever and disease.

Thus Lawrence slept, many and many times, convincing himself of his folly's rightness. More lunatic than Lear and more weary than Ulysses, he was closer to wishing his death than his return to base. The war's end was going to be his own. He was left with his contempt for flag and empire while he had tried to serve both. His mental self-flagellation would only lead to the actual mortification of his flesh. Pain was the only pleasure he would allow, the only feeling he could welcome. Nothing would often seem closer to ecstatic orgasm than pain and, in the meantime, nothing would be so alien to it; in fact, unless paradise condescended to become hell, the two would never meet.

He had seen the peripheries and borderlines of bleak immensities, the burning out of the energies of men of steel. Now, the century is dying and carries with it the millennium's death. No fin-de-siècle charm for us, just an apocalypse, like Lawrence's demise.

Sand storms turned the blue of his eyes into red and insomnia caved his cheeks into his face. Thus an imperialist revolutionary opened the first paragraph of this bloody century. The book was written with everything but words, I would say with bones, blood, and instruments of torture.

The sun was still young and Arabia calling. While we have lost our fury, Lawrence's rage was new. He could have run, in Damascus's dark alleys, into Rimbaud's standing ghost. When we will bid farewell to this millennium we will have become unable to question some of Love's most celebrated failures.

One thinks of you, Lawrence, now that your language is practically unreadable. Time has sped away. We are today more involved with galaxies than with our own earth. Since its beginning the century promised us destruction, and you said it to Yorkshire's winds and in the coded messages that you meant for the Indies. Listen, Arabian graves bear no names because these are in God's remembrance. The turquoise skies drown in the Red Sea. We're so heavy with sleep, already. Comets do illuminate our hearts but, as you know, the heart is seldom meant for triumph.

The desert. Pure space spread for the imagination's drive. Animals created themselves in order to move. Movement is more essential than matter. The mind is a desert mirroring the empty stretches of Arabia. To kill is a meaningless action compared to the effect of the Rub al Khali's climate; only the sky with its dust of stars can measure itself to it. No people would be indigenous to such a furnace: only a God intolerant of all other deities could inhabit this overheated and desolate landscape; everybody else is a stranger.

The mind is seared and acquires the attributes of light. The knowledge of emptiness is a precondition for love's existence and for its understanding. The spirit blows over sand dunes. Mountains do walk in the Hedjaz. In the early morning the world ceases to be what it was the night before, and only a faint notion of the universe reaches one's consciousness. Travelers—if there are any—are in constant search of water. Empires crumble while being built. The spirit is humiliated by the sun. The only lakes one can see are hallucinations. Therefore, the spirit easily breaks loose, all inner boundaries transgressed. The passage is operated in full light. Insanity becomes normative and memories are taken for projections into the future. Water becomes the object of sexual desire. The self ignores when it was born. Light stays in infinite immobility. Then from one second to the next it vanishes. By then nobody knows if the darkness is of the soul or of the world.

Mes pensées cannibales, Lawrence used to think in his dislike of the French. Mental and physical pain were so fused in him that they were, ironically, reuniting his broken self while making him wonder if the earth did indeed belong to the universe. Nothingness soothes the mind. The human will bends and releases its venoms but the target is ever-shifting; Lawrence's broke, not against stone but against some strange reflections on the sky's surface. He couldn't survive on absinth and thorn. His ultimate enemy became matter's alliance with movement. Armies turn into phantoms in such an environment. Neither war nor peace are

(57)

elements of the desert, only minerals survive in that mineral world. In there, stone pyramids, not made by men, point to the spirit and crush it with the very energy that elevated them.

Lawrence was a permanent lie. His love was for violent death. He yearned to sit in the midst of a mind cleaned out of every possible desire, and he succeeded. He reigned over one of history's most thorough destructions; over the dead body of his love.

The desert creates, simultaneously, addiction and withdrawal. Its air is always rarefied and espouses one's body. One doesn't think in terms of life or death when one is facing its rose-colored cliffs or saturated yellows.

One summer in Piestany, I was helping a World War II concentration camp survivor cross a garden she couldn't negotiate. She asked me what I was reading in that hospital and I said that it was *The Seven Pillars of Wisdom*. "Oh!" she said with a frown, "Arabia! A dangerous place." "Don't worry," I replied, "it is not. It doesn't exist." She must not have comprehended that we are ourselves geological sediments left with no ancient concepts which will come to our rescue.

Yes, the desert is compulsive as a result of its magnetic forces that become demons when one remains unaware for too long.

Great and numerous armies died of longing on waterless and sun-drenched expanses. Also, men produced by the Nile's canals and mudflats meet their misery on the gravelled wastes of the Sinai. Fire rains on their backs. Lawrence died much before the tragedies he helped engineer became operative. His own engine crushed him under the English weather. The clouds of his death's horizon watched with no feeling of pain.

He was a figure drawn on the sand. The desert gnaws at the spirit and pushes it into desperate action. Inland sea, it is a killer. Everything else is torture.

The air fills gradually with memories of English places. He sees rain where there's no water and grass. He floats back and forth over inseparable realities with a sense of the growing evidence that he's crossing Arabia on camelback. His headdress is thin protection.

Now he's seen from afar from multiple points of view because nothing around him is fixed. Lying on territory incessantly sculpted by winds, his own visibility, so to speak, is at night, when the stars shine with mercy. He will try to reorient himself, there being nothing else to do.

There is an erotic quality to his weariness. Ascetic in regard to his sexuality, he spent few exhausting nights in his youth. His transgression into the Arab side of the world was the mirror image of the experiments to which he submitted his body. Now, everything in him quivers: his knees, mainly, his lower belly, his buttocks, besides his heart and dispersed spirit. He knows he will not last long because all his schemes are part of a larger concept of betrayal.

The sunset was all encompassing, and as he was welded to the world, he took it to be a confirmation of his uniqueness, the sign of his resurrection, as he was used to live ahead of himself.

There was perfection to the mirage: the sand was blue and streaked with the irisations of a sea. Still, he felt reassured of not being back on English shores. At this sterility's end, the stars took over; sleep was not coming and the little boy he had kept within himself started to count them as if they were marbles. A thin line was separating his mind from the heavens, the line of awareness. Toward the morning he cried for mercy, but his pride was quick to rebel. He dismissed everything. Only in total denial could he find a semblance of peace.

He loved this pain, this punishing, his body twisting with thirst, panting like a stray dog in the middle of a circular and barren plateau. Mother earth was at last his sole enemy. He welcomed the stones' company because they were resigned to their kind of thirst for millions of years. Wherefrom this primordial fire that was burning him without claiming him once and for all?! The horizon was advancing and Christ College stood in front of his vision, rising through transparent smoke and undulating under the overflow of rippling beer. He started hearing his old college buddies' lewd songs but there was nobody, nobody was ever going to exist, neither Arab nor English, neither human nor animal, there was only his own soul going up in flames, and ash. . .

Bedouins found him unconscious and dehydrated. Picking him up like some laundry left behind, they deposited him on the floor of an abandoned outpost. Some shade and murky water brought him back to his private torments. Pain had transferred his self to this form of death that he was so desperately seeking. Night of night, night's end and end's night.

All the missing things—the world—became his obsession, obsession with the fact that he didn't miss them. Then, what? Why were they staring at him? They wanted to be rejected—like him—acknowledged and refused, emblematic of what everyone calls life.

Space on the desert is not to be filled either with material or immaterial things. Matter's own reality becomes dubious. It's not the air that one breathes—he always breathed with difficulty, as if air were thick, to be swallowed—which concerned him, but whatever pushes beyond air, a substance more tenuous, volatile, unstable, something like spirits thinned out by the mind's intense attention.

*

Pain. You have to give it a name, in your sleep, in your unawareness. But pain is pure awareness. Of itself. Circularity is of its essence. But it is not pure geometry or, if it's pure geometry, it's one inscribed, branded on skin and flesh.

Pain is both the journey and the traveler, a traveler who doesn't live side by side with you but within you. The more this traveler becomes you, the less you can travel. At point zero both elements are perfected into becoming one and you become this startling thing: the supreme traveler for whom immobility is the perfect condition.

This reality belongs to the realm of the invisible. It resides there, forcefully, eating up every other form of being in the body, and yet you cannot touch, smell, or hear it. That's why it has become in some times and spaces a "spirit," an angel, an angel of good or evil. They said it redeems, finding an excuse for it. They said it's a devil, a material spirit that needs to be exorcised, extricated from the body, sent to its companions in hell.

Pain is neither masculine nor feminine but rather androgynous. It's mean, it gets at your moral fiber and does much more. It bends your knees as easily as it plies your will.

People state their pain, cry, shout, howl, whimper . . . or whisper their acute discomfort, but pain itself remains silent, ominously so. Silent (like water in its most dangerous state, before it forms a river), it gets absorbed, turns us into sponges, porous bodies, a porous body within the old body.

Pain is expressed in ways alien to its reality. It is a pre-language or non-language event, one of matter's manifestations; matter oozes pain and the body picks up the message, a message of its own making. In this narcissistic, and supremely pessimistic, encounter, we do not play a role, we play host.

It is born in live cells. We descend with it toward a nucleus, which isn't there, which is less than empty space, a void. So pain resides in voids and fills them with its unsubstantial substance.

We try to describe it to friends and doctors and they look puzzled before sending us back to our suffering condition. Where is it, they ask? And when you place your hand on where it *hurts*, you know that it isn't there, it's nowhere because it is non-spatial and, although it has duration, it isn't in time either, being only in a perpetually present tense.

Does pain, therefore, resemble love? The temptation to equate them would be great, as they so often bring each other about. But it is not because they're inseparable that they're alike. Then, what to say?

Love and pain somehow function in similar ways: they do not give us a break, absorbing all of our attention. They each become our inner and outer landscapes, our identity. We possess them and become possessed, using similar terms for both: we look for a cure, or a way out, speak of oblivion, rest or panic, even death. Both maladies wrench the heart and pull ligaments apart. Each resides in every cell of the body and of the mind, separately and jointly.

In solitude, pain brings hallucinations. Out in the desert, its power makes columns of marble rise. Thirst fills one's mouth with dust. One ceases to talk, language gets reduced to a few words, a few sounds, and then to mere breath.

The body is not supposed to know itself, being an instrument for the apprehension of the world, not unlike our eyes, which are not meant to see themselves. But the body knows itself in apocalyptic moments: in ecstasy, and in pain. During intense sexual pleasure we are flesh and volume, belonging to an intense here and now, muscles mobilized, the skin stretched, the inner energy radiating. The body illuminates the space it occupies, turned toward a single direction. When the object of one's desire is absent or removed, the same phenomenon occurs, but transformed into pain, a symmetrical and negative image of that ecstasy. The body creates then by itself a situation that is—to itself—unbearable.

Lawrence: short, woman-like in his Arab clothes, neither a transvestite nor an actor on this foreign land's too-empty stage. Yes, he became speed in the early days of airplanes, he became dulled—with passion—in the first decades of this century of horror.

He did not encounter crime on these miles of wilderness, but the profound friendliness of the Bedouins who protected him as they would a child. They knew he was transient, like everything, the way their Revelation said.

His will, though, did not appear to be transient; it was monolithic. A single stone rolling. From where to where? From his English mind's depth to his dreams of conquest.

In his pain he achieved a strong sense of his being and this, mostly, when he knew that he was sliding toward his own end. In ordinary times he was numbed, in a state of sweet madness. He was casting his shadow over the twentieth century, in passion, in betrayal.

Looking beyond the open nothingness which was confronting his mind as well as the receding movements of the skies, his eyes were desperately trying to hang onto some shape, some form, but he could only hear the wind's whistle and a few sounds that were spilling through his throat: it was similar to those moments when desire creates unnerving, both painful and vacuous, like a reservoir that contemplates with terror its last drops of water trickling through its gigantic faucets.

He had to finally disinvest his body and his soul, and crush whatever was left from his will and attain the point where his spirit would at last triumph over this orgy of self-destruction.

The greatest part of this infernal work was already done: S.A. had died and all Lawrence could do was to describe the young man's rotting away. His endeavor—to create and disintegrate an empire—was already rendered futile. He had not been defeated but, worse than that, he had been betrayed by those who set him on his dreams. To die or to destroy. To write *The Seven Pillars*, to transfer totally his self into the writer's.

*

Mental pain resides in the heart. Lawrence's reality had reached the logic of dreams.

I see his face, once more, in the mirror, his body lying in dust. He's both alive and senseless. It is not the rape in the Turkish prison that made this pain but the place of that event in a broader landscape of falsity that was the core of the humiliation endured. He is crying now in the wilderness, both thanking and cursing the ancient gods of Arabia who still control the God of all monotheisms.

There's nothing in the desert save the desert itself and this is true of the passing of Time. Red sediments, exploded granites, scorched patches of clay, these were the elements among which he experienced eternity's apocalyptic apparition.

Betrayal constituted the thread of this century and love was the other thread, a love reduced too often to the measure of its absence.

Betrayal carries love into pain's darkest regions and is never redeemed. Love's object dies first and then betrayal kills the lover slowly and surely. The story comes into a void.

Lawrence is in a state of pure consciousness. Clouds are so rare, so fluid!

There's no tomorrow in the skies, nor on the desert. No past and no future. This century made it sure that the next one will be permanent permanence, will live an immobilized sentiment of the present. Nothingness is that which only death makes possible.

Yes, he brought toward himself "a tide of men," but they never reached any destination. True, the conquest of the desert is the most erotically rewarding experience, but it opens on illusion.

Lawrence went to where Arthur Rimbaud preceded him by one generation, but both, knowing that the land they visited was the territory of desert Arabs, resolved that these were creatures of the wind and accommodated themselves with a strange empathy. Would the wind erase the haunting memory of the betrayal?

Confronted with the demons of betrayal and the desertification of the history of the people whose downfall he helped bring about, Lawrence felt the urge to dissociate his soul from his body as an inescapable temptation, the urge to give in to the angelic desire.

The price to pay—a Faustian one—was for his self to die to itself and to the world, and to carry into that annihilation everybody and everything.

The century whose ending we are now witnessing dreamed that dream and paid that price, the perfect alibi for the destruction of paradise.

V PRESENT TIME

PLACE
Then, I had wanted to return to the forest. Cork oaks were extending their arms to greet me. I found a path and followed it. The trees extended their blackness over my head. When I reached a fountain, I felt thirsty and I drank, cupping my hands. The trails went further; so did I.

WEATHER
Under the shade provided by the oaks I rested for a while. My breathing relaxed. I tried not to sleep but as I had lost track of time I think that I must have gone to that other world into which sleep takes us. I don't remember having had a dream but I suddenly noticed that the sun had covered a long stretch of the sky and had left me disoriented. The forest's temperature had been affected. I needed a jacket and I didn't have one, so I went on walking. All along the walk I was hearing water running, but the sound was not strong enough to be created by a river.

MY HOUSE
I was away for a week and happy to have left my belongings behind. In the forest I started to desire a house that would look like a cabin, and be built with redwood: I needed the reddish penumbra and the fireplace. But where should that house be? In Maine? On the blue ridges of Virginia? No! It's too early for me to leave California, although I spent half a century in it. My ultimate house is California itself, a state for which I feel a passion that is a good match only to my

love for the sea. The only eternity on my horizon is made of that particular land and of its seas. I will disappear in an absolute sense if and only when they disappear.

A PERSON
This forest, which is mine for the time being, behaves like a woman: it awakes with the singing of birds and opens its windows to the morning light. For the rest of the day, it takes in whatever happens, with some detachment. It has known floods and fires, so there's little left of what can disturb its easygoing temperament.

WIRES
The size of the trees isolates my trail. But the trail itself is a thread that may lead me to terror: we are not in Crete, and the Minotaur is nowhere to be found, but nothing is sure when it comes to the world of the unknown. I have had a desire for fear, strangely enough, too often not to be rewarded. If the Minotaur were to be waiting for me I would be willing to follow him in the forest and, even further, in his imagination.

THE CHURCHES
Architects get their inspiration from forests. They use them for their constructions, but also use their soul. Any structure has also to do with the forest and its trees. The very idea of a shelter is given us by interlocking branches, and sacred places such as temples or churches charted in their hushed shadows.

MY HOUSE
A house is the seat of one's impatience. The elements I'm most interested in are the void, emptiness, framed spaces, passages, I mean doors and windows. Walls usually disappear from my memory, or, if they linger, turn into wavery surfaces, moving patches of pale colors.

POLITICS
Roses can give lessons to politicians: their beauty is protected by thorns; they need pruning for survival, and their

love for sun and clarity is proverbial. Their power resides in their fragrance.

PEOPLE
I see them arrive in busloads and I wonder: who are these men with bulging bellies who behave in the open the way they do in their barracks? The women who accompany them do not make a better impression. Their skins have no fur and they don't prick up their ears at the slightest noise. They all talk high and loud. Wherever they go they think that they are in Central America.

VITAL DATA
A hare went by and I foolishly tried to follow it in its quick run to the fern.

I enjoyed the light that was not coming from a single source but was rather diffused, that was not stopped by any object but was covering it with its gentleness. I was immersed in an environment in which I was radiating my own electricity and where physical boundaries were made flexible.

EDUCATION
When I'm happy I go to the beach, or wish I could. When my friends arrive too early, I put on Monteverdi. When I re-read Plato, I erase everything else.

BUSINESS
To be a writer is to be chained to a table, and to be waiting for a complacent wave, and when it arrives, to ride on it, and then align on a piece of paper, or on a screen, a series of words, with the belief that they are of serious importance although knowing well that with the current of change all the things we do or say will be totally obsolete before the century's end. But let us not sink into depression. We have to distill our anguish and spill it with much care on all kinds of surfaces until the hour of total incapacity.

MY HOUSE, THIS PLACE AND BODY
I need not repeat my need for windows, and when a window has been opened I feel the urge to travel, and when at the airport, I get nauseated until my plane takes off, and when I land, I dread police and customs, being overwhelmed by a sense of guilt, then, when in the taxicab I start hoping that my hotel room will not be too claustrophobic. Once in that new room, I go to the window and look out and worry about the narrowness of the street below. I usually take a shower in what reminds me of old telephone booths, then lie on the bed. My imagination turns in circles and the city already looks dull, already predictable. If I came specially to attend an opera I begin to wonder if the performance will be good enough to justify all the trouble I went through.

THE SAME PERSON
The trail was going uphill and getting narrower, and I first hesitated, then walked until I reached the forest. The forest took me into its womb; it felt comfortable, spiritually rewarding. My fears were alleviated, my limbs now felt weightless. I looked for little animals but didn't find any. I picked up little stones and threw them, just to hear the sound they made. The forest was getting thicker. At a certain moment I looked for the sky and I couldn't see it and I wondered if it was still daytime or if the night had descended in all its majesty. I stood for a while. It was so peaceful. I had to make a decision, so I decided to return to my starting point.

WEATHER
The rain was descending softly on the leaves and branches. One drop at a time. It looked like dew gently settling. Pine needles and other dry leaves were crunching underfoot and were establishing conversations with the surroundings. No easy return in view. I will need days and nights to reach the end of this journey.

PLACE
On this Easter weekend sleeping accommodations are all booked and filled, and the idea of spending the night in my

car is quite unpleasant. But the night is beautiful. I'm in a California desert, and it's a day's ride from the forest. The stars are all out. I have a hard time separating one constellation from another and the whole show is blinking and sparkling. Not knowing much about astronomy, I just gaze at all these celestial bodies that, for me, have recovered their mystery. I ignore where I am and if I am. The stars have transferred my consciousness to themselves.

MY HOUSE MY CAT MY COMPANY
I haven't seen Fujiyama, and that hurts, hurts deeply. My cat died recently and, there, I didn't feel sorry. It's true that I went through some activities that would have indicated that I must have been miserable, but I was not. Still, to please my friends, I arranged for a small and intimate funeral ceremony. I picked up a shoebox, and Jenny came with a bunch of tulips and a single rose, and we went, well, we went . . . to the Sausalito dump. There, for no reason that I know of, we both started to cry.

POLITICS
I am both an American and an Arab and these identities are sometimes at odds with each other, not every day, not even often, but once in a great while I become a mountain that some terrifying earthquake has split.

MORE VITAL DATA
It's not about the ocean, it's not about the whale, it's not about Ahab, it's about America's psyche.

And it's not about democracy, it's not about oil, it's not about people, it's about a child gone crazy with power.

And it's not about history, not about suffering, not about the universe, it's about pure motion pushing ahead.

EDUCATION
How does one make paper airplanes that fly over the seas, propelled by their own will? Until I make one, I will con-

sider my ignorance to be unfathomable. I will also love to reverse the time machine and meet with the Pythia of Delphi and ask her to prophesy the fate of the Greeks after the conquest of Troy, or Byzantium's fate after the passage of the last horse mounted by the last drunken crusader.

In the meantime we store memories like neurotic folks do with empty bottles and faded magazines.

In Turkey, village women embroider roses on black silk, in order to stop thinking and remembering.

BUSINESS

These women wash their clothes by the banks of a river. I watch them steal happiness from the running water and spread it over their hands. They bend their knees with pleasure, stretch their arms the way they do when alone. Back in their homes, they smile to their kitchen pots that they have made to shine. Long cotton threads measure their days, and during the night their dreams bring them all the things that daylight has refused.

THAT SAME PERSON

Possession of the world: One of them accepted an arranged marriage with a Yemenite worker from California's Central Valley. They had no common language but that helped the young husband during his wedding night. He didn't have to invent sweet sentences, and she confused her fear of being possessed with her inability to talk. At a certain point, he beamed because he experienced the proof of her virginity. He called this night "the night of the conquest." The heat of the Valley was mild compared to his passion. As for her, she could talk to herself in her own language, and what she heard was rather strange: she was thinking of the chickens that her father was regularly decapitating in front of their house's door, and of the little streams of blood immediately sucked by the road's dust. As she remembered the penises of her numerous brothers, at different ages, she giggled, comparing them to her husband's menacing and hard virility. "I have a man,

(72)

not little siblings," that's what she told herself, not without some pride. And like a cat transported into new surroundings, she started sniffing, observing, measuring and discovering the beginning of a huge continent called America.

WIRES

The sun is very low this evening while I'm watching cows on the road to Drake's Beach. When the mind is free, it can see that a cow is a mountain. These magnificent structures move with solemn grace.

By the road's end there's the ocean and I am torn between its appeal and the fascination to which I'm subjected. The cows start coming toward me. They can turn a sane person into a demented one just by the power of their walk, which, in a moment, can become a ceremonial stampede. Cows and oceans share a kinship. I realize that, getting entangled in their kind of reality. I take from my car a pair of sturdy scissors and cut the wires, and the cows, as in a corrida, pass me by inches and pour themselves onto the highway. They will reach the beach before me.

WEATHER

In the rain forest everything was young. I looked for clouds, to no avail: the sky was green and made of branches. I couldn't think of music, the slightest sound being already ominous. I shouldn't, though, create a misunderstanding here; there was no terror to this forest but an incredible freshness that no music could ever provide to a soul.

I'm in this forest and moving through the trees on its soft, fragrant floor. I'm moving with no effort, set for no particular orientation. The air is soft, too, and enveloping, friendly. I'm breathing with my body, my skin, air being a light and benevolent substance. In here, trails do not become labyrinths but remain openings. A slight humidity humanizes, renews energies. It merges me with the thin redwoods and the baytrees that grow by their sides in a network of vegetal bodies and limbs. I don't know where I am but I'm not lost; I'm rather attuned to the workings of this micro-universe.

PLACE

The island's history is stormy: Seven young princes had fled to a cave at the foot of a nearby mountain. As they were holding a star in their hands they thought that they had entered heaven and that they were within divine light. In the meanwhile, waves of soldiers were sweeping the inhabitants into the water, putting fire to their homes. Their turn came to disappear into the sea. Stunned by the racket, the young princes turned their cave into a sealed shelter. They met a dreadful death. No boat has, since, ever been able to lower its anchor in this place.

PEOPLE

I have an eagerness to linger on the past, and calm my heart, which is these days beating too fast, but instead of reading history books I find myself buying maps. The most recent one I bought is of Turkey.

To live on San Francisco Bay and be looking at a flat image of Turkey is rather a difficult thing. It's the coastline that interests me most, but I mistakenly picked up a map of ancient Anatolia filled with Greek names of fabulous cities. It's useless to play games with oneself! Sitting by a lamp in front of a large window that allows in the whole of Mount Tamalpais, my finger searches for Smyrna, one of the seven destinations of John The Evangelist's Letters. So, I can define the nature of the sacred terror with which that city's name is endowed. I also know that it was occupied by the Venetians in 1472, having heard my mother say it each time she wanted to explain the Italian name that her Greek father and ancestors kept throughout centuries. It's true that Venetian rule lasted very briefly and that Tamerlane's conquest of the region was of greater importance.

Smyrna is by the sea but always destroyed by fire. It seems that the gods are still playing at the old game of lighting fires all over the eastern Mediterranean. Lately, they took sides in the latest war in Lebanon and complicated matters enormously. They keep planting seeds for the archeologists of the future.

From Smyrna I push north to Magnesia, and Perganum, and Assos and Troy! But tonight Homer is looming big and I feel tired. I will watch the news on TV, or pay a visit to Joe Bacon, across the street. I'll buy some other map tomorrow: I'll have to anchor myself, somewhere in deep water, before too long. For the time being, Sausalito will do, as it has always done.

HOUSE, MY BREATH AND WINDOW

I told him: take me to your house. A few seconds later, he said: "all right, let's catch the streetcar."

At the right station we came out on a narrow street with messy sidewalks. We walked a bit, silently, stopped in front of a wooden door, then went up the stairs to the first floor of the building. He took his key out of his pocket and opened this second door, which let us enter a rather large living room with a checkered marble floor. It was a cool space, aerated, with sparse furniture. I sat, and he sat facing me. We were not at ease. "Come and see the kitchen," he said, and I did go and saw pots on a shelf, and a stove. It smelled like all kitchens: of rosemary, garlic, onions, cinnamon . . . but lightly so.

"It's so clean," I said. We crossed back into the living room and went out on the balcony. I looked at a passing streetcar, at a few cars, some people on the sidewalk. I returned to my seat and he followed me.

"The maid isn't here to make you a coffee," he said. It didn't matter.

"I have had enough coffee for today," I said, and he remained silent.

I noticed that he was breathing with some difficulty and thought that he looked tired: we had exams during the whole week. There were no paintings on the walls but a few framed family photographs. Oh yes! a plant was growing in a large orangey container. A philodendron. How funny, I thought.

"You wanted to see my house," he said, "you haven't seen my room." He looked shy, like girls would usually do in such a situation. His room was rather disappointing: like a room in a not too expensive hotel and after the maid had done it.

"Who makes up your room?" I asked, and he replied that it was his mother who took care of the house . . . So he had lied about the coffee and the maid. He showed a great embarrassment and I regretted my visit, I felt that he would have liked to be rich and impress me with things like beautiful rugs. I realized that he was sweating, although slightly.

We were standing in that room, awkwardly, when he sat on his bed, first, then touched my arm, pulled me toward him and obliged me in a way to sit next to him. I passed my hand over the bedcover and the cotton was coarse. I wanted to leave.

He tried to unbutton my shirt and I objected, he put his arm around my shoulders and I disengaged myself; then he brought his face close to mine and I had to discourage him from going any further. He bit his tongue. He told me that it was time for him to sleep with a girl and I didn't answer. He was becoming nervous, and I was staring at the door. He said "I love you" in a hushed voice. He must have thought that that was the way to start a love affair. I made it clear that I didn't want any lovemaking, no, not today, and probably not tomorrow. He felt humiliated and hesitated between being violent or sarcastic. I gazed into his eyes and they were pale. "Then why did you want to see my house," he said, "come all the way to my room, why?"

We were used to taking the streetcar after one of our classes and cross the city back and forth, talking loudly and laughing. We were probably playing lovers. But now, in an empty house and on a comfortable bed, I was hampered by a

(76)

primeval fear of rape even if I was being asked to give in with great gentleness, with some despair, some deep urgency.

"A girl doesn't come into a boy's bedroom of her own will if it weren't with amorous intentions," he repeated. I took his hand in mine, held it, and noticed the moisture and the trembling and I put a kiss on his sleeve and said that that was enough. . . A thin layer of haze covered his gaze and I felt at a loss. I cried, I mean tears welled up into my eyes. After a short while, we tried to laugh, knowing that the storm wasn't going to break out.

POLITICS

When, in 1874, J.F. Glidden took two wires and twisted them together, he invented barbed wire, emblem of our civilization. He intended it to keep sheep and cows safely on their pastures for the benefit of Midwestern farmers, most of them immigrants to the New World. In the process, and to start with, this barrier destroyed Native Americans' social organization on the Plains where they were free to move, hunt, and gather. Later, this simple device came to signify trenches and camps. Haven't we seen images of human flesh scattered on their spikes like debris from a shipwreck? Much more, these wires have become models for all the invisible lines that separate people, nations, continents. The longest barbed-wire frontier is the one that runs between rich and poor nations, and politics has turned into the art of keeping this stretched line stretched as long as possible.

FINAL VITAL DATA

I do not paint apples, I draw inkpots. I do not climb mountains, I sit in cafés. I don't travel but buy picture books of exotic places and I do not swim, but write about the sea.

EDUCATION

What did they teach to samurais? Courage, I think. Courage—when, for what? For dying warlords? For social order? For the drama of committing hara-kiri?

What did the Maya tell their children? We don't know; there's therefore a big hole in our education. We're responsible for the disappearance of the Aztecs, Mayas and Incas. The beast in us doesn't care.

Our prosperous countries have the luxury to teach children facts about rivers, mountains and other places they don't see, and that's not only a waste of time but a dangerous practice because when they are confronted by the genuine things they will not be experiencing the sense of discovery.

I am, though, intensely curious about planets, stars, galaxies, comets. As there's no way to visit them, my only link is their names, their distances from us, their degrees of luminosity, their patterns in the sky.

I had once the good fortune to transcend ordinary knowledge. It was on August 11, 1999. I witnessed the sun's total eclipse from Pension Nonntal's garden in Salzburg. During the duration of the whole event, I let myself be invaded by a celestial phenomenon of incommensurable magnitude over which any power was abysmally nonexistent. I lived within a fraction of an hour a dawn and a twilight totally independent of the normal day in which they occurred. That cosmic event pulled us out from Earth and took us somewhere both secret and nonmaterial.

ANOTHER PERSON

Something moved in the forest. I searched in my immediate vicinity and all I could find was a squirrel, high up on its tree; it couldn't have caused the commotion coming from under the fallen leaves.

Who has gone ahead of me on this trail? Now I'm walking silently and mysterious questions are facing me with insistence: why have I come to this place, why did I resign from my job to take this trip? Am I really the child of those I called my parents? What will happen by the road's end?

Does digging into memories ever appease the heart? A tidal wave of images from my past engulfs the forest: this young girl is descending from the Jack London ranch in Glen Ellen, followed by awesome Jersey cows. It's just after her brother's suicide, committed on the premises. He veered off the road into a ravine while driving his truck and they didn't need to take him to the hospital: it was too late.

This young girl, later, insisted on becoming a boy and upset the family. Her mother was horrified at the idea of her daughter refusing her gender, and the former young lady became an unhappy young man.

In the forest, I'm looking for Mr. Shepard, the young person's grandfather, as I had spent many Christmas dinners with his family on the ranch, while the children were excited by the mountain of toys laid under the tree. That little girl who was, in the future, going to make them so unhappy, was the youngest. Once she was crying and beating her older brother with her fists, and he told her that if she were a boy he would have smashed her with one blow. "Then I will become one," she said.

At the end of the ranch there was a forest of firs and redwoods, and, in the spring, a roaring creek. I am hearing this creek, right now, and it's probably the cause of the sounds and stirrings that I just heard.

THE FIRST PERSON

There's a bed with a copper headboard, surely bought at a flea market. I love its Japanese bedspread made with the special indigo-dye cotton that is Japan's signature. On the right side, there are, against the wall, shelves made of cherry wood, from floor to ceiling, with art books at the bottom, and for the rest . . . well! In front, and between windows, there's a dresser with drawers, some filled with personal papers, some with Indian jewelry, mixed with underwear, scarves and sweaters. Nobody uses this room, nobody, and hasn't for a long time. I moved recently into the house, using the other rooms and facilities, waiting . . . I have the premonition that the first person I will see entering it will faint, or scream, or die.

HOUSEHOLD APPLES
Apples bring to mind flowers. That's the way it is. Flowers attend weddings as well as funerals. For a dinner, a few will do. Three roses at 9 p.m. always look good.

I took some apples from my kitchen and put them in a brown bag. Was it because of Cezanne's apples or my uncle's orchard in the old days in that Syrian valley where he was spending his days, and certainly his nights, with his second peasant-woman wife.

I offered them, with earnest application, to "her," in her pension, a room she was renting while visiting me in my little town, having come from Paris. She opened the bag and saw the colored objects, not seeing all the other things, that is, the thoughts and the passion that I was bringing with the apples. She was disappointed—she probably hated apples—and I sensed that, and sensed that at that very moment I became unworthy of her love.

CHURCH
If you take the altar, the candles, the pictures and the people away, you will be left with the knowledge of an unnamable disaster.

BUSINESS
Where are we heading? Having access to an unlimited number of words within any language, and to remarkably intricate sets of language games, we still stumble on sentences we can't finish, on ideas we can't express. Musical instruments, paints and paper all cost money, but words do not have a market price. Then, what happens to thinking?

Turning away from a world over which I have no hold, I entirely give myself to the present time, in its most mineral sense, in its immediacy. For instance, I'm happy today because it's the longest day of the year, summer's formal beginning. What amuses me is that I felt autumn's presence in the early afternoon in spite of this formality; there was a breeze within the heat, a coming through of cool air that, added to yesterday's soft rain, lopsided the season. The weather is having fun.

I'm in Paris, asking silly questions, such as: why is France a foreign country? Then, when darkness comes, I look for stars which aren't there: they don't visit this city too often. I think of California and that's a good enough occupation. Since I live in an apartment with no view of sea or mountain, my mind wanders as far as it can, but it has acquired habits and it invariably lands me by a sea or an ocean. It's clear. I travel at will to the Pacific or to the Mediterranean with no tickets, no airplanes, no nothing. Sea and ocean are closer than the room next door. They replace books. They keep my attention fixed on them. They focus my thinking on questions: What's the sea's nature? Is there a metaphysical difference between the sea and the ocean? Can one, by penetrating her waves, decode her secret? Is she just waves in movement, mass of water, or a strange being with fits and convulsions? Ask her.

Outside, it is "La Nuit de la Musique" in Paris, and the night is sparkling black, with lingering visibility, and I apologize; I'm not in a foreign country, music being a place of origin. People are pouring from every street and corner. I move with the crowd, there's dancing, noise, and even pockets of silence in this pandemonium, this festive explosion.

VI TIME, DESIRE, AND FOG

PLACE*

After many peregrinations, multiple sunsets and endless sunrises, I ended up in B. . . , a harbor with no moorings, just a bay in the southern Mediterranean; in fact, we crash-landed, some passengers and myself, with no casualties. We spent the night in a WWII army outpost, surrounded on all but one side by the desert, the other by the sea, another wilderness. The wilderness—and the wildness—were in my soul. It felt good to be for a whole night between a rejected past and a lack of purpose for the future, where a swift and decisive battle had taken place: history has its skies and lightnings; it can strike and leave no trace.

WEATHER

From Benghazi to Beirut, away from my home in California, away from Mount Shasta, cold weather becomes pure memory. In Nature's calendar, flowers dig under a crusty sand for drops of water. I would like to ask them if they know what goes on in their realm. But of course they know. There's an adequateness here between blood and air, skin and shadow, passion between life and planet Earth.

MY HOUSE

Open doors, open seas, once in a while an open heart: dwellings. Do I sleep in a cube of white flames or between walls of running water?

---

*Benghazi, Libya.

One's unavoidable house is the body. Sometimes, this primeval house is some other person's body, loved, or despised.

A PERSON

We're never left alone because of the way memory functions. The will calls memories into focus, but they acquire independence, moving forward or backward, they consume us, they hide or refuse to serve our frustrated minds. When they turn into witches, they eat directly into the brain, leave us breathless, then bloodless, on the floor. What's left of the person is carried—often accompanied by long processions of people—to a couple of square meters, where it will soon start to feed the clay of the soil with its non-usable organs.

WIRES

To be honest, I must say that it was awful to watch a friend of mine in whose head they had plugged wires. By the time they convinced me that the electricity was well connected, that the whole beneficial system was working well, I had begun to faint. When I woke up, I felt a violent headache, and I screamed.

THE CHURCH

When I see a church on every street I wonder how it will be possible to think freely here. But alas, in this little hill town, we *do* think. (With dismal results.)

MY HOUSE

"Let's take the car," I said, that fateful day, and in spite of the warning emitted by the radio, "let's go to our mountain house!" Simone said yes. We left Beirut and drove along the coastline. I noticed the waves and the wind. Then it started to rain. The car was turning into a bathtub. (I'm exaggerating, I know, but it *was* full of steam, making it hard to drive.) With her sleeve my friend kept wiping the front window. I was doing the same with the window on my left. The wipers, outside, were as frantic as we were. We were moving in a world overtaken by water. The wind blew ferociously. The car swayed. At a familiar landmark we turned right, finding ourselves driving east. That road is sinuous. We went on for a good hour. Through the snowy rain, the wetness, I was trying to get a view of the mountain range, against which stood the village that was our destination. But the Barouk refused to be seen. Following the custom of those women who still veil themselves, it kept its face invisible. Invisible also like some Imams of the Islamic world, or even like the Platonic Ideas that float around waiting to be unveiled.

The car entered the cedar forest. The trees looked forced to stay where they were, agitating their arms. As they were making thick shadows, we put on the front lights and the road caught fire under the wheels. The night was material. We were moving in it like in black foam.

We came out of the forest's heart and the trees were sparse and the road had to go down before climbing again. It was a steep section of a narrow strip and we suddenly saw a Jeep ahead of us. The rain was pouring hard, mixed with snow and wind. It was mesmerizing to see the heavy vehicle slide toward the right and I knew that it was going over the edge and deep into the valley, and I was hypnotized into following it, and in a quick moment, anticipating its fall with a clear mind and no emotion, telling myself that they were all going to die and that probably I would lose control of my own car as well. By some improbable luck, the Jeep stopped on three wheels and we slammed into it and I hurt my knee and my wrist. But I kept going, and for the rest of the drive I felt embarrassed at not having felt any worry, any sorrow, about what looked then like the certain fall of the vehicle ahead and the certain death of its occupants. I was quietly waiting for the catastrophe to happen, oblivious of the fact that fascination was making me follow them to the end. "Where are we?" Simone asked, waking me from these thoughts. I looked ahead and saw, through the rain and snow, that we had just reached the hotel that is a few hundred yards away from my mountain house.

POLITICS

My terrace is lined with Italian clay pots which contain different species of plants. A rose bush is growing beautifully in the largest one, capturing the morning rays of light. The roses affect my heartbeats with their fragrance.

My neighbor, though, installed on his own terrace huge barrels planted with little firs. In a few years, a small forest was blocking my view!

I'm sad, I'm desperate: a place that was splendid, and envied by all, turned into a prison, or, at least, into seclusion. This is what people do to each other.

PEOPLE

We are in the month of Ramadan, a month for fasting and prayers. From my high-perched terrace I used to see in a panoramic sweep the summits of the Barouk, Sannine and Djebel Knisset. On a clear day, of course. My neighbor has denied me this pleasure. If it weren't for the fear of imprisonment, I would have killed him. Yes, life's sanctity stops at the threshold of whims and interests. I can send somebody to blow him up in his car, while he drives to work, but this kill-by-hire business has a way of backfiring.

VITAL DATA

The price of coffee went up. Anne-Sophie Mütter is playing Vivaldi's *Four Seasons* in this large apartment. I don't dream of California in green anymore but in yellow. The Mojave Desert is getting ready to receive nuclear waste in great amounts within a month. In Paris, the restaurant on Rue de Vaugirard by Rue Madame has closed. Whatever is closed is not open: radical closure. The earth is round and doesn't intend to become a square. When I was up there, with Neil Armstrong, the moon looked flat, but the earth was jumping and tumbling over the horizon.

The charges on my apartment are being inflated. Too much money for too much fuel for too many guards. I can't move out: they hemmed me in. But I'm left with iridescent roses and I'm going to buy a watering can and water them, day after day, come rain or sunshine.

EDUCATION
I understand how the muezzin's last call to prayer spreads within the sky and sinks in the direction of the mounting darkness. I'm losing my hold on the sliding day, and sitting on a chair seemingly firm, I feel that I am engulfed by an invisible wave that is carrying me into this geometry we call "the world," and also into something else for which we do not have a name.

BUSINESS
That little cove has a little boat. I used to go swimming there when I was six or seven. Back then it felt protected (nobody cared by whom or from what). Innocent years of our lives! In the late seventies that corner of town exploded when the nearby American Embassy went up in flames. The cove shook, its wooden (and rotten) structures floated on the sea. The devastation is still visible. The ground of the Embassy is now a (thriving) parking lot. The little café and the cabins nearby, where we used to undress quickly, are now covered by a permanent pile of garbage.

MY HOUSE, THIS PLACE AND BODY
Living in different houses doesn't mean living in one for each season. And does home still mean bed, kitchen and mailbox?

This room in which I process my thoughts along the turbulences of my soul, has a wall-to-wall window that lets in the sea and the sky at their darkening hours. I hear the evening call to prayer that covers centuries. This near lamentation turns language into a desert chant. The sun has gone under. The desert is at my mental door because Beirut is a special kind of a wasteland. It defies our means, belittles our intelligence, defeats the will. . . . Once this is said, its mystery unfolds, its beauty too.

(87)

THE SAME PERSON

Jamal Naufal was flying to Riyadh when a fierce sandstorm forced the plane to land in Jeddah. It was at dusk. Some passengers had relatives in the city, others looked for hotels. Jamal Naufal was telling me that he had decided to hire a taxi all the way to Riyadh. A young man, about his age, was standing by, looking perplexed. They looked at each other, liked what they each saw: a decent traveler stranded at an airport by the Red Sea.

They talked and agreed to share their ride and cut expenses. They immediately guessed, by their similar accents, that they were both Lebanese, so they relaxed comfortably in the back seat. Exchanging a few words, they soon discovered that they both worked for the same company in the heart of Arabia.

As they knew that they wouldn't arrive, at best, before the early hours of the morning, they each tried to sleep. (Jamal Naufal didn't remember much of how time went by on that trip. His story was being told during dinner and over many drinks, in summer, in his village in Lebanon's mountains. The air smelled of pine.)

They slept neither for long nor well. They started a new conversation. Jamal Naufal asked his companion what his name was and the guy said: "Jamal Naufal. And you?"

Jamal Naufal was startled. It was still dark and the car was racing on the beams of its own lights. The road looked smooth and eerie. They could have been still on the airplane.

He gave his name. The other Jamal Naufal was startled too. They scared each other. They knew it wasn't a lie. They exchanged the dates of their birth. They were born the same year and same day. Now they avoided looking at each other, each fearing to turn into some sort of a mirror facing a mirror.

(88)

When at last they arrived in Riyadh they discovered, by giving instructions to their driver, that they had booked themselves into the same hotel.

The clerk at the Riyadh Intercontinental was confused. He did have a reservation for a Jamal Naufal, but it was for one person, one room, and one key. He said: "Yes sir," looking once at the one, then at the other, "how come you're two people?" And probably because he had been raised in India, he added: "Sir, did you by any chance bring with you your Double?" For a split second Jamal Naufal wondered if the clerk wasn't right. Jamal wondered too. He was dead tired.

WEATHER

We drove to Sidon by the sea, the only way to get there. It was warm in the car, the heater producing a mini-climate for two. At some point I pushed a button and pulled down a window. Cold air rushed in. What pleasure can such air bring to an overheated face! I hesitated for a moment, fearing I might catch the flu if the window stayed open for too long. The sound of the sea followed the wind's. It wasn't too strong a wind but I didn't want to take any risk. I pulled up the car window the same way I have closed out, so many times, so many things from my life.

PLACE

We looked—Youssef and I—for a soap factory which is being restored, and that search made me realize that I didn't know much about this little city and that I could easily lose my way through its complex network of narrow alleys. Sidon has about nine miles of souks, medieval roads lined with shops, narrow even for a bicycle. The merchandise spills over and, between the plastic wares and the people, one can hardly move. We are far from the covered markets of Aleppo or Istanbul. Sidon's alleys are narrower than anywhere in the world, and forgotten. This city, though mentioned some seventeen times in the *Odyssey*, is of no interest to anyone but to itself, and that makes it a wonderful object for discovery. What could be more interesting than to discover—uncover—like an archaeologist who's also a futurist, a place only twenty miles away from the one in which you were born!

PEOPLE

They were strolling through the recent ruins of Beirut; she was speaking of the Swedes as if they had invented the cinema, recalling *Persona* and *Wild Strawberries*, insisting on the fact that she had watched them when she was a student in the sixties, in Berkeley, in a garage turned movie house by a woman named Pauline Kael whom she never forgot. She was of course much older now, but she had fallen in love with the guy she was walking with. He told her that he never went west of New York . . . It occurred to her (was it because of the summer heat?) that he was going to die one day, and that it could happen soon. . . . "When I die," he asked, "please be quick. Muslims don't keep a corpse for long." "I will not let them take you," she replied quietly, "I will keep you to myself as long as I can. Don't leave me!"

Her panic started to invade his spirit, too. Thoughts were running behind his words like reels of film: once dead, he wouldn't be able to come back and help her in her grief. He was stuck: he had to go on living.

They reached a nice hotel downtown which has at its thirteenth floor a bar with a view and, all night, they drank beer after beer.

MY HOUSE MY CAT MY COMPANY

How to separate the self from the non-self? This question may never find an answer, but it can assume different forms. Was I already a cat when I identified the first cat I encountered? Only the same knows the same, I've always thought.

Whatever keeps us company is an intrinsic part of the awareness of the self, and isn't the self the awareness of itself?

It seems that there are exchanges of personalities, in the depths of the self, between humans, animals and objects. Beware: don't touch that glass of water in front of you. You can, when drinking it, become water and spill on the floor and mess the rug . . . and have to apologize to your host.

POLITICS
When gods thought of themselves as being humans too, the latter fancied that they had become gods. Ever since, there has not been peace either in heaven or on earth.

MORE VITAL DATA
Description of the harbor. Of the site, the mountains, the hills. Description of the bluish snow, the rarefied air. Of horizontal clouds. Of the sky's brilliance, the sunset's reflection on the mountain's panoramic side. Of the names: Sannine, Djebel Knisset, Dhour. Description of slow summers, of the overwhelming of one's soul by splendor. Description of springs surviving among rocks, of waterfalls benevolent toward goats, of lightning striking trees. Of petrified beauty and stranded travelers. Description of a shepherd's eye on a girl's blushing, of fog, of moon rising over divinities. Description of clear air and muddy thoughts, of the waiting, the wake, the want. Description of that which never starts and of that which never ends.

EDUCATION
It's always a matter of repetition and castration, obedience and rejection, learning and forgetting, of approximations and codified laws, of salvation at the price of destruction.

BUSINESS
Of windows on a lone tree, dreams of future kisses, a matter of posters with pierced stars, hunger for more chocolate and less bread, of forays into another child's pocket, of long hours under violent rains, sloshing shoes and galoshes, clouds moving across blackboards, of the single bed in the coldest corner of a room.

THAT SAME PERSON

And now, listen: We stopped at some intersection in a frightful traffic jam. The vehicles are drab, dusty, cranky, running chaotically in all directions. As visibility was nil, the roads full of crevasses, I worried. A river of people was filling the streets thickly and moving steadily. Where is the factory?

We take a wrong turn and move at a snail's pace in an alley obviously unfit for cars. The shops overflow with goods, dresses, shoes, and . . . sweets! The Orient's ingenuity in making pastries is here at its height.

I left the car, even though it blocked the passage, my frustration becoming unmanageable.

I know that I am pursuing a no-exit situation. There are dimmed lights ahead, thinner crowds, a growing silence. I keep walking. My friend Youssef is following.

Now, I am alone and the alleys turn into a labyrinth. It's getting really dark in here. The pavement, made of smooth stone, feels like soap. I can still see the walls, which are touching my shoulders. I'm nearing panic but holding, holding my breath, and my fear. The only escape left is my imagination, and it is catching fire.

I continue on my odyssey. I am probably below ground level, and searching. . . I am Orpheus.

I hear music. Why does Orpheus need music? Does music enlarge the imagination's limits? Does it dilate our senses, transforming the smallest space into an ocean? Orpheus plays music and sings: In his case, ordinary language becomes lead.

He's vocalizing ancient Greek folk tunes. He's crying. The labyrinth is hearing not a song but a lamentation. Orpheus realizes that he has entered a forbidden city, and that Eurydice resides further below, in the abyss, in the unknown.

His search continues: he's of divine essence, but to no avail. He advances with arms stretched, groping for a ghost who's preceding him in a realm not yet in his grasp.

Why is Orpheus persisting in his doomed endeavor if not because he knows that it is too late? The labyrinth he entered is a one-way run. It collapses behind anyone who dares to walk its tunnels.

He can only keep going, calling Eurydice. His reason is faltering. All that's left to him is his imagination's shadow that leads him into more darkness, more despair.

Now the labyrinth has entirely collapsed. There's no trace of it. The light that I see above its former location is deadlier than the void.

WIRES
A witch tells sinister stories to children such as the one about a person who was outgrowing his shoes while counting numbers, or about another who was dislocating mountains by the sheer fact of looking at them. All the parents living in the neighborhood got together and resolved to shut her in her house. They sealed her front door with little metal threads.

WEATHER
With old age comes winter.

PLACE
The little courtyard is terraced in Roman fashion. It is surrounded by fig trees. There are also, a bit further, crawling vines. The floor is paved with flat stones that are streaked with pink hues, as if much wine had been poured into their grain.

PEOPLE
This young man is new to you. Your senses are refreshed by his presence. You want to take in, like a thief, like a whale, like a lover, everything that he's giving you.

(93)

HOUSE, MY BREATH AND WINDOW

The conversation with the people from the past who just exited has exhausted me. I wish they would never return. But then, will I be condemned to spend the rest of my life looking at the world through my window? Right now, all I see are patches of sunlight.

POLITICS

His image mixed with the colored clouds of the evening, a man is lying against the trunk of a magnolia tree. His woman comes with a bowl of rice. He's sure she loves him, and smiles, but all she wants is to mate and kill.

FINAL VITAL DATA

Confusion spreads easily over continents, and questions of identity dissolve in the tubes where our will is put to test. Heat waves rise and destroy our ability to use our limbs without suffering. We cling to the memory of lightness. We yearn for lemon and kumquat trees.

Do not believe, we are told, the habitual tales of jealousy. The engines have been shut off. The quietness doesn't promise the coming of an exuberant crowd. All around, decay is visible. Visible, also, triumph.

They wrenched the still-beating heart out of its cage. We wished time to be accelerated, we got thrown away against a tree.

EDUCATION

If I needed the perfect proof that one's house is one's prison I would take Malaparte's house in the Bay of Naples. We know that it was designed by the writer according to the plan of a Sicilian church and built on the island of Lipari, where he had been imprisoned for five years on Mussolini's orders. It is itself an island on an island. On an impregnable hill-rock Malaparte secured his windows with iron bars.

Standing there one learns with unbearable clarity that the most open-sea landscape fast becomes the most oppressive element of isolation that one can experience.

ANOTHER PERSON

Orpheus was running a music store, selling videos to adolescents and sometimes projecting, in a back room, pornographic movies for adult maniacs.

One afternoon, a young girl entered the store and asked for Glück's "Orpheus and Eurydice": he found the CD and showed it to her. His hand touched hers and they both blushed. They looked at each other intensely. They felt petrified. They were shaking with emotion. At last, she broke out of the spell. Taking some money from her purse, she paid and left.

He looked and looked into the space she had just occupied and became struck with terror.

A strange warmth overtook his body. He had to get out. He threw himself into the street, having locked his shop.

He walked aimlessly for quite a while. He then visited a few music stores, went to the seafront, recognized a few fishermen. His vision started to tire. People, cars, buildings, all superfluous, he thought.

He entered the old quarter of Sidon, its miles of alleys. Walls were turned into waves because his imagination was on fire. Waves were turning into flames. He found his pace in this alternation. He picked up the *nay* that he had taken with him when he started his journey. He started to blow gently into his instrument.

The alleys by their endlessness affected his sense of orientation. The labyrinth was sucking him in. He went on making music. The music was wailing. He was begging God to help him.

He heard no answer, he gave up praying. He felt utter lone-liness.

He played a tune from Glück's "Orpheus. . ." and called "Eurydice! Eurydice!" The walls trembled and the sound's echo was drowning his mind. He entered a realm of no-return, a passage to nowhere. . . His very search, he told himself, was creating the impossibility of ever encountering her again. In his last act of remembrance he remembered that every loss is a descent into hell.

THE FIRST PERSON
In the meantime, she had gone home and deposited the CD in a drawer; she had turned the key.

She drove to the edge of the forest along a long road that took her to the mountain. It was a clear September day when she entered it.

She welcomed the trees and their freshness. They were cedars. She entered the forest with the certitude that nobody would follow her there. She found a trail but gave it up for uncharted spaces. As she continued to walk, the for-est was getting thicker. She heard sounds, but they couldn't be music . . .

She desired to keep the image of the young man of the music store alive, vivid. She heard Glück's music in her head and thought that an opera is a forest, each tree having at its tip a voice, a word, a sound.

She fell asleep. The idea that she would eventually die of thirst and hunger didn't bother her. The forest was probably the promised paradise, she thought.

After a few weeks—or so it seemed—she felt weak. Some water and a few berries hidden under the cedars were bare sustenance. She admitted that it was most likely that she would never hear the music she had bought.

The young man was accompanying her through her imagination. They did live together in the forest, in the strange way of his absence. The word love frightened her. It was too ominous.

It was too late. If he found her now, it would be a dying woman he would find. If he brought her back to life, it would be to live next to one who knew death . . . and death forever would be between them, like a plague that would contaminate both. This young woman that she is would be branded with the sign of doom.

Her attention was then awakened by some noise, some smoke, the stirring of pine needles; a dark cloud flew at ground level, and she realized that there was a fire, that the forest was burning, and that she soon was going to burn and be reduced to ashes and disappear, leaving no trace.

HOUSEHOLD APPLES

Dionysus squeezed apple seeds into lethal wine. He drank the funereal potion and before dying he had a vision of young women tasting, and shining, like the poison-carrying fruit that we casually eat.

CHURCH

The dramatic and rather hopeless search for the past haunts our nights and obscures the present. But I crossed oceans just to catch the remembrance of a certain Easter day of my childhood. I walked the street leading to the school around the corner from my house, sat in a café with my head bent on my hands, looked endlessly at the sea, let my body sink in fatigue and pain . . .

Suddenly, one day, the breeze flew horizontally, touched my ear, surrounded me; I shivered, my heart quivered, made itself forgotten, then I felt soft and bodiless, weightless, lost sense of self and non-self. I became pure living substance, indefinable existence, and the breeze changed direction, blew softly to the opposite side, and it brought Resurrection, brought that particular Feast intact in its setting and weather, in the present of my soul. I experienced a simultaneity of past and present, I lived the miracle of being a child and an adult, innocent and yet hyperconscious, I was in April and in December in some absolute reality which was no abstraction. The weather itself appeared to be like the Spirit in Greek theology. I was breathing in air as a child and as an adult, in a climate redoubled into spring and winter, like me, all of this already gone by the time it was noticed.

BUSINESS

On this Ramadan's last day it's business as usual. But the fast has drained bodies and souls. The merchants are happy to close shop, go home, and feel saintly.

VI TO BE IN A TIME OF WAR

To say nothing, do nothing, mark time, to bend, to straighten up, to blame oneself, to stand, to go toward the window, to change one's mind in the process, to return to one's chair, to stand again, to go to the bathroom, to close the door, to then open the door, to go to the kitchen, to not eat or drink, to return to the table, to be bored, to take a few steps on the rug, to come close to the chimney, to look at it, to find it dull, to turn left to the main door, to come back to the room, to hesitate, to go on, just a bit, a trifle, to stop, to pull the right side of the curtain, then the other side, to stare at the wall.

To look at the watch, the clock, the alarm clock, to listen to the ticking, to think about it, to look again, to go to the tap, to open the refrigerator, to close it, to open the door, to feel the cold, to close the door, to feel hungry, to wait, to wait for—dinner time, to go to the kitchen, to reopen the fridge, to take out the cheese, to open the drawer, to take out a knife, to carry the cheese and enter the dining room, to rest the plate on the table, to lay the table for one, to sit down, to cut the cheese in four servings, to take a bite, to introduce the cheese into the mouth, to chew and swallow, to forget to swallow, to daydream, to chew again, to go back to the kitchen, to wipe one's mouth, to wash one's hands, to dry them, to put the cheese back into the refrigerator, to close that door, to let go of the day.

To listen to the radio, to put it off, to walk a bit, to think, to give up thinking, to look for the key, to wonder, to do nothing, to regret the passing of time, to find a solution, to want to go to the beach, to tell that the sun is going down, to hurry, to take the key, to open the car door, to sit, to pull the door shut, insert the key in the ignition, turn it, warm up the engine, to listen, to make sure nobody's around, to pull back, to go ahead, to turn right, then left, to drive straight on, to follow the road, to take many curves, to drive down the coast, look at the ocean, to admire it, to feel happy, to go up the hill, to reach the other side, then go straight, to stop, to make sure that the ocean has not disappeared, to feel lucky, to stop the engine, to open the door, to exit, to close the door, to look straight ahead, to appreciate the breeze, to advance into the waves.

To wake up, to stretch, to get out of bed, to dress, to stagger toward the window, to be ecstatic about the garden's beauty, to observe the quality of the light, to distinguish the roses from the hyacinths, to wonder if it rained in the night, to establish contact with the mountain, to notice its color, to see if the clouds are moving, to stop, to go to the kitchen, to grind some coffee, to light the gas, to heat water, hear it boiling, to make the coffee, to shut off the gas, to pour the coffee, to decide to have some milk with it, to bring out the bottle, to pour the milk in the aluminum pan, to heat it, to be careful, to pour, to mix the coffee with the milk, to feel the heat, to bring the cup to one's mouth, to drink, to drink again, to face the day's chores, to stand and go to the kitchen, to come back and put the radio on, to bring the volume up, to hear that the war against Iraq has started.

To get more and more impatient, to be hungry, to bite one's nails, to wear a jacket, to open the door, walk down the hill, to look at the Bay, see boats, notice a big sailboat, to go on walking, to be breathless, to turn left, then right, to enter the Sushi-Ran, to wait, to look at the waitress, to call her, to rest one's elbows on the table, to pull them back when the tea arrives, to order, to eat, to drink, to use chopsticks, to be through, to wipe one's mouth with the napkin, to read the bill, to count, to pay, to thank graciously, to exit, to start the road uphill.

To rise early, to hurry down to the driveway, to look for the paper, take it out of its yellow bag, to read on the front-page WAR, to notice that WAR takes half a page, to feel a shiver down the spine, to tell that that's it, to know that they dared, that they jumped the line, to read that Baghdad is being bombed, to envision a rain of fire, to hear the noise, to be heartbroken, to stare at the trees, to go up slowly while reading, to come back to the front page, read WAR again, to look at the word as if it were a spider, to feel paralyzed, to look for help within oneself, to know helplessness, to pick up the phone, to give up, to get dressed, to look through the windows, to suffer from the day's beauty, to hate to death the authors of such crimes, to realize that it's useless to think, to pick up the purse, to go down the stairs, to see people smashed to a pulp, to say yes indeed the day is beautiful, to not know anything, to go on walking, to take notice of people's indifference toward each other.

To have lunch. To ask for a beer. To give one's order. To drink, eat, and pay. To leave. To reach home. To find the key. To enter. To wait. To think about the war. To glance at the watch. To put on the news. To listen to the poison distilled by the military correspondents. To get a headache. To eat dry biscuits. To put the radio back on. To hear bombs falling on Baghdad. To listen to ambulances. To go out on the deck. To look at the lengthening shadows on the grass. To count a few dead flies on the pane. To go to the table and look at the mail. To feel discouraged. To drink some water. To not understand the wind. To wonder if the human race is not in chaos. To wish to blow up the planet. To admire those who are marching against the war.

To hear a war from far away, for others. To bomb, eliminate a country, blow up a civilization, destroy the living. To exit from one idea to enter another. To go. To cross the Golden Gate. To enter San Francisco. To stop at the light. To enjoy the luminosity of the green. To be on Market Street. To see too many policemen. To be told to keep going. To see young men being arrested at the end of the march. To measure tension in the air. To seek Valencia. To go all the way to Connecticut Street and park the car. To enter through the gate of CCAC. To sit in a room which is dark. To listen to a poet, then to another, speak about a time gone.

To stop at the gas station and fill up the tank. To go uphill, peek at Mount Tamalpais. To take a rest, breathe, contemplate. To find a path and walk on wet grounds. To enjoy the enormous variety of the shades of green on the mountain. To raise one's eyes to the sky and bring them back on the horizon to compare the different greys of the sky. To try to speak to the clouds. To say yes, it's impossible. To linger on the mystery of communication, to bemoan its absence. To say it's okay, then not to believe oneself. To think of the morning news, to be horrified. To despise. To hate. To empty one's head of overflowing emotions. To regret that evil exists. To blame oneself for the existence of evil. To want to forget about it and not be capable of so doing. To wrap oneself with death.

To turn the page without moving into a new life. To put on the radio. To listen and to be hit in the face with much poison. To curse the hour, the fire, the deluge and hell. To lose patience. To lynch misfortune. To prevent the trajectory of inner defeat from reaching the center. To resist. To stand up. To raise the volume. To learn that the marches against the war are growing in number. To admit that human nature is multifaceted. To know that war is everywhere. To admit that some do win. To drink some water. To turn in circles. To pretend that one is not spent out. To believe it. To pretend. To discuss with one's heart. To talk to it. To quiet it down, if possible. To curse the savagery of the technologically powered new crusades. To remain in doubt. To come out of it in triumph.

To run down for the Sunday paper. To read: "Target: Baghdad." Back to the radio, hear about the American dissidents. Hear that the Blacks are overwhelmingly against the war, that the Iraqis are resisting. Do some cleaning. To put up with an inner rage. To admit the evidence of evil, the existence of pain. To not be capable of finding one's source of energy within. Feel gratitude for those who protest although knowing that they are moved by their own moral sense. Take risks, that's what they do. To think that the Arab states feel uncertain, to say the least. To find the radio unbearable.

To wait for the reaction, the vengeance. To be thirsty, hot, then to feel cold. To invade the body, says evil. To speak of evil. To make a phone call. Not to tell all that one thinks. Not to think about all one knows. To hang up. To pick up the bottle of Correctol and start erasing memories. Not to be hungry but to eat, nevertheless. To satisfy other needs by eating. To feel disgusted. To count the dead on either side. To come back to the radio while congratulating oneself for not possessing a TV. To listen to the Egyptian, Turkish, Jordanian, Syrian and Iraqi reporters on the radio. To feel worn out.

To admire the light, bless the spring. To bring down the garbage, close the lid. On the way up, to look at the blue-bells, smell the verbena and the sage. Once in the living-room, hear and weigh the silence. To suffer from the disaster. To do nothing. To think about history then reject that thought. To align some books on the shelf, and throw out quite a few. To pick up a magazine, to throw it back into its basket. To find a forgotten translation of Parmenides. To read a few sentences, discovering his impatience. To intend to read him later, but there's no "later" at this moment. To consider the present time as sheer lead.

To put things in order. To find a 1975 diary. To read at random: "Back from Damascus." To read, further: "Sunday the 12th. Mawakef meeting." To leave the notebook on the table. Turn the radio on KPFA. To absorb the news like a bitter drink. To create terror, that's war. To wallow in cruelty, conquest. To burn. To kill. To torture. To humiliate: that's war, again and again. To try to break the iron circle. To go downtown at least, to park on Caledonia. To walk all the way to the Valhalla, along the water. Measure the mast of an extraordinarily beautiful sailboat with one's incredulous eyes. Admire the black hull and its thinness. Compare the lightness of the sailboat to the government's moral thickness. To admit that there's nothing that one can do.

To bring down a military plane over Afghanistan. To welcome the sun. To water the plants. To roll back the hose. To unroll it again. To go on watering. To place the hose next to the wall. To displace shadows while displacing oneself. To go back to the typewriter. To worry about the ribbon, to wonder if it needs to be replaced by a new one. To control the desire for sherbets. To breathe painfully. To keep one's anger low key, sweep away one's worries. To take off the shoes and wear other ones, and enjoy the result. To see what time it is. To uncork the inkpots. To read "Mont Blanc" on the label. To fear the ink will evaporate. To carefully close the inkpot. To glance at the watch and realize that it's time for the (bad) news. To put up with it.

To read on the calendar that Lynn Kirby is coming for lunch. To discuss the atrocities committed by the British and the Americans in Iraq. To hear her say that war is an atrocity, point. To speak about astronauts and Space. To discuss the possibility of a collaboration. To bring to the table roast beef and salad. To mix the salad. To look at the mountain. To later bring down the night over the mountain. To guess its presence through the night. To affirm love, look through the void, measure its depth. To wonder if it is permissible that some eat bio-foods while others die of hunger. To imagine the war in Iraq. To intimately know how ferocious invading armies ate. To try not to die of hatred. To hold one's head between one's hands. To press on. To close one's eyes. To have difficulty breathing.

To destroy Baghdad is the order of the day. To hear the soundtrack of the war. To be stunned by the spring's colored beauty. To have coffee at Da Vino. To shake and sweat at the sight of a woman who is a walking skeleton helped to a car. To buy cornbread at the Real Food Store. To feel guilty when thinking of hunger. To be back. To admire the garden's incredible beauty. To go up and store the bread. To turn the radio on. To find the official hypocrisy untenable. To repeat that they are war criminals. To feel a lead-like fatigue all the way down the body. To be desperate. To know the absoluteness of the war. To still believe that the future will escape the diabolical schemes of the enemy.

To extinguish the light in the eyes of those who love the world, to threaten life itself, to impose death, that's war. To pour blood in the Euphrates and kill the inhabitants of the Tigris's banks. To displace hills. To wipe out an open market. To make it impossible to get married, to sleep, to get up one morning in Bassorah, while they do such things in other places. To meddle with Arab destiny. To anticipate the deaths, the wheeling and dealing. To pray to the ancient gods. To not despair about the past. To not forget. To be sure that someday, no one knows when, justice will prevail. To know that the world will take revenge for having been fooled. To keep knowing that there are mysteries and secrets.

To dream of deserts, to count the cactuses and all venomous plants.

To yearn for spectacular suns. To raise one arm, then the other. To follow the uninterrupted flow of news and reach an unbearable level of sadness. To pretend that one is okay because of the hunger in the stomach. To not eat or keep time. To pick up the notebook, then put it back on the shelf. To live with the knowledge that the Americans, the English, their allies, want the people of Iraq, the children, the men of Iraq, to be destroyed. To compare what's going on with what has always been going on. To hang by a straw. To be disoriented. To be running and standing still, in the dark, on the deck. To read the map of the sky. To mark out the stars. To spot the Pleiades. To remember Babylon. To spread blackness over one's heart. To come in, to close the door. To wait for the slightest noise. To put an end to a long day. To go to sleep.

To do as if things mattered. To look calm, polite, when Gaza is under siege and when a blackish tide slowly engulfs the Palestinians. How not to die of rage? To project on the screen World War I, then World War II, while expecting the Third one. To scare the innocent, by following the Israeli way of spreading terror. To make a phone call to Paris. To tell Walid that things are all right. To lie. To admit that the weather is noncommittal, beautifully. To feel indifference toward a spring suddenly heating up. To choose which shirt to wear. To fill one's mind with the apprehension of the Sunday paper there, at the door.

To read a lot of trash mixing the blood of war with business's stench. To root out any happiness. To go out, and down, and on the road. To hesitate; to go on, and ahead, and back, and up the stairs, and in one's room. On the way, to notice that the mountain is still there. To lie and sleep, deeply, heavily. To reproduce night's sleep. To wake up, look through the window at green water, from the Bay to the mountain, and return to one's self. To remember that war is devastating Iraq. To feel pain.

To walk toward the chimney, stand there, return to the table, sit and uncork the inkpot. Bring the cork back to its place. To follow a shadow's edge. To raise one arm in order to create a shadow. To not define its color. To be puzzled by its nature. To mentally cover distances and not decide if they are on earth or in space. To hear steps. Prick up one's ears. To wait. To put uncertainty to rest. To evacuate the brain from any sort of presence. To get rid of that guilt while doubt starts to creep in again. To fix one's eyes on the painting. To get lost in the painting. To make coffee. To pour it but forget to drink it. To drink it cooled down, throw out the rest. To get upset. To say the hell with it the hell with it. To wait for the mail while thinking who cares?

To go to the dentist early in the morning then drive back and come home. To lie down, waiting for the news at noon. To have a headache. To be impatient. To vomit the war. To greet the fog with joy, with tears. To find tenderness in stones. To greet Sarah Miles, with tea, with cakes. To miss the news. To chat. To say goodbye. To start packing. To forget the war. To never stop thinking about it. To ignore the beauty of the day. To water the garden. To slobber with disgust. To notice the porcelain blue of the sky. To follow a cloud. To encounter other blues. To come back to Earth. To fly over hills. To feel the breeze. To read an invisible line that says in Baghdad people die ferociously. To face the mind's emptiness.

To fly heavily like a crow. To hear the wind. To ply the branches. To blow one's tree into the wild olive tree. To read Heraclitus. To call him "the obscure," because his thinking happens within the questioning of clarity. To read Heidegger, soon. To be informed by a phone call that Turkey is stirring over Iraq. To witness the execution of Iraq. To force the Arabs to move backward. To be moved by the beauty of Rhea Galanake's poem. To not feel in good shape. To be getting old, to fight anxiety. To think about the trip. To visualize oneself at the airport. To start counting the days. To yawn. To look through the window. To measure the extent of one's sadness, while denying its power. To look for the latter to no avail.

To rise in the middle of a feeling of discouragement. To make coffee. To warm some milk. To take vitamins. To wait for the storm. To listen to the news and let oneself believe that things, later, will be much better. To find little energy in the body or in the mind. To distill thoughts like one does alcohol, a drop at a time. To remember green plantations, red earth, black faces, white tears. To recall that nothing seems to have changed. To face a profound weariness. To stop the flow of these defeatist considerations. To keep quiet.

To land in New York. To pick up the baggage, climb in a taxi, cross a bridge, drive into the red sun, enter the city, stop at 90th Street, take the elevator, leave the valise on the floor, lie on the bed, stare at the ceiling, forget it all. To go to the Saigon Grill a few hours later was a pleasure: to order eggplant and rice, to pay, to go back to a deep sleep. To feel in the morning the hostility of humid weather, to wonder why the trees are still without leaves, to follow the branches all the way to their tips, to realize how high the surrounding buildings can be, to start counting the wall's bricks.

To sneeze out the pollution. To rub the soot off the mirror. To cough and spit. To buy the *New York Times* and find it disgusting. To look at pictures glorifying war. To be appalled by the number of civilian casualties. To feel ashamed of feeling so comfortable in the apartment. To feel tired of living. To betray one's thoughts. To have a drink and too much food. To love beer, and the Park. To plan a trip to the Metropolitan. To decide to walk through the Park while . . .

To call California. To submit to much disinformation. To bring the bottle close, to drink Evian. To be embarrassed that Bassorah's inhabitants are dying of thirst under the returning British. To die of thirst is for the natives. To die is for others. To inform the living that they aren't yet dead. To hear in children's voices their future death. To dim the light, with restlessness. To go to the kitchen for no reason. To sit in the dark. To welcome dark thoughts. To loosen the squeeze around one's heart. To empty one's veins of all forms of love. To find oneself inanimate. To be immured.

To sneak through the hours. To fall into prostration. To get lost in questioning. To close all avenues. To let dusk fall or, rather, shadows climb. To light the lamps. To avoid the news. To wash one's hands. To dry them carefully. To shake one's head and everything inside it. To breathe with difficulty. To not worry, but be bored. To reach a state of parallel awareness. To go to the window just to make sure that it's very sad outside, like in Baghdad, under the bombs. To wonder why one is so placid. To be accused, by the angel, of being so ready for compromise. To foresee no personal action. To remember that it will snow, unusually. To dread the evening. To go to Steve Lacey's concert.

To anticipate trouble. To go down Second Avenue, exit on 10th Street, enter The Barracuda and sit, facing fish-and-chips. To eat in a hurry. To enter St. Mark's Church, buy a ticket. To listen to a clarinet player. To recognize Douglas Dunn against the screen on which his dancers become shadows. To applaud Steve Lacey. To be worried about the bandage around his head, his swollen cheek. To realize that his tempo has slightly slowed down and that his music is somehow crying. To take off one's heavy jacket in the over-heated room. To let Steve's music invade the place. To use the program sheet as a fan. To hear the pounding of Baghdad in the music's tissue. To wonder if Nouri will stay alive through this war. To come back totally to the music. To find it barbaric, ecstatic. To mix the soprano sax with the dancers. To mix the dance with the deep-seated knowledge that things have gone wrong.

To wake in the morning in a snow storm. To be surprised that it's happening in April. To remember the flowering cherry trees from former springs. To drink the coffee while it's still hot. To go out in the cold and buy the paper. To put on new shoes. To hurry back and throw the paper into its corner. To contemplate the snowfall under its silver sky. To compare a tree to a Christmas tree. To go out again, this time for lunch at Edgard's. To order salad with smoked salmon. To pour oil and vinegar. To call the waitress who comes and pours coffee. To find that the coffee is black, like the world.

To desire strongly to be in Baghdad, in defiance of the war. To taunt danger. To know that the end is near. To halluci-nate. To see the amputated like vases set on shelves. To hear shouts and press one's hands over one's ears. To shout. To answer the phone which inadvertently stops the night-mare. To make tea. To find out that the water is tepid and the hour is sour. To thank the sky for having stopped the snow. To think of Beirut, dream of Palestine, miss Baghdad, be reminded of the impossibility to be ever totally where one is. To despise history as taught, but love Greece anyway, always. To need the celebration of courage. In the single room to put out the light. To look at the spreading evening is inescapable.

To speak of angels according to oneself and according to Rilke. To evoke Malte Laurids Brigge. To remember one's adolescence and fear the distance. To suffer. To still love those one has loved. To discover that one has really loved. To wonder if remembering things past in open air is less painful than this imprisonment. To have a bad taste in the mouth. To bite one's nails. To feel pain about Iraq. To revolt against the torture to which it is being submitted. To have stiff joints and lumbago. To cross the day like an acclimated ghost. To lose sight of any reason to be.

To not underestimate mathematical functions. To expect them to reestablish some direction for thinking, for exploding dormant certitudes. To chase despair away while knowing the futility of such an endeavor. To gaze in wonder at cruelty. To interrupt some invisible process. To greet friends. To hear them coughing. To say that we eradicated small sicknesses and kept the big ones. To project the interior image of Baghdad. To remember the 1976 trip. To spend days in Baghdad, in dream, in remembrance. To be shot back to New York, in a daze. To drink water to push down a bufferin. To be swelling. To look at nowhere, in prostration. To renounce both hope and surrender. To edge toward nothingness.

To search one's memory for the past's residues. To indulge in insomnia. To snow on the reservoir. To scrutinize the sky, fly from branch to branch, cut through air a passage to tall buildings in a pink morning. To go and buy the paper where some reporter affirms that to bomb Guernica, Rotterdam, Baghdad or New York ends up being so many crimes of war. . . . To hear the phone ring, to look at the snow, to meditate on cruelty while there's noise in the corridor. To smell the neighbor's cuisine. To be obsessed by food as a substitute for . . . what? To catch a glimpse of one's childhood.

To transform matter into spirit. To cross the threshold. To abolish all signs, then go after them. To decode the future. To rust. To wonder how to digest defeat instead of vomiting it in the middle of the night, and go back to one's bed and pull up the covers. To try to be convinced that New York is an interesting place. To throw a disillusioned glance at the courtyard, to call that a garden! To be exasperated and leave for the Park. To try to avoid little pools of melted snow. To stand under a tree and try to count spots of snow on the trunk. To admire light yellow broom trees. To follow a trail. To slow down, returning to 90th Street. To enter left, then right, push the button in the elevator, fetch the key, enter . . . enter a void.

To sweep the living room in order to disperse all the cluttering angels. To think of California, which is receding. To be bored. To release into the air a vision of Baghdad disappeared. To lose energy on anger. To encapsulate the present. To be agitated in order not to be more restless. To give way to the body's floodgates. To observe intensely the pictures of Iraqi corpses lying on their land. To wish the end of everything, oneself and others. To return to those images and transform them into icons. To pray.

To move forward into parading indifference. To bury one's feelings. To feel relief at the hairdresser. To stroll. To clean out some memories and allow death to manifest itself. To project the movie of things that just happened, let bitterness invade the soul. To fight regrets and lose the battle. To know that when it's nighttime here it's early morning in Baghdad. To think of Badr Shaker al Sayyab. To descend into his tomb to inform him that Bassorah is being destroyed. To wash blood off its people's faces. To leave Badr to his sleep. To fly back to New York the indifferent, the wounded. To remember Innana's poems. To call Babylon's gods. To wish that

(111)

they join the fight, and know that that won't happen. To foresee vengeance in death.

To face the iridescent inner chaos. To start a grey day. To lose the limit between the self and its environment. Buy two newspapers in order to double the horror. To reach the bottom of horror. Turn distances into a tunnel. Receive a package. Read Bobby's letter predicting worldwide cataclysm. Believe him. To enter Time's movement. To walk around the block. To remove wet shoes. To watch one's heartbeats. To give up writing the letter, give up everything. To need some sleep. To swallow the pill. To wait for Ruth and Annea. To let the body do the thinking about the war.

To buzz with fatigue. To dream (almost) of canals and planted fields. To climb mountains, but it's not true. To be glued to the ground. To hurt because they are hurting. To bury the living dead. To lower one's mask. To clean the bathtub with disgust. To feel guilty and blame it on the war. To be puzzled by the enormity of what is happening. To live in a kind of luxury, avoid the idea that it could be different. To wait for the end of that which will not end.

To lift the great song again but then see that Saadi Youssef has not received his entry visa, To believe that democracy has become a charade. To rest has become useless. To prevent light from reaching the spirit. To warm one's resentment. To wish a non-ambiguous farewell to presidential palaces. To collapse. To hear steps. To go to the door, let a friend in. To speak of the weather then slide into war news. To find them bloody and monotonous. To fail to bring one's attention to something else. To insist on violence's bestiality. To say goodbye to the friend. To err in a closed space. To alter one's perceptions by pain's sovereignty. To ask death to be accountable. To hope that the Tigris will not slow down.

To measure the mirrors' depth, drain their blood and fill them with water. To drown in them, to render one's glance uninhabitable. To enter a heavily destroyed city of Baghdad.

Read on the calendar: April 9, 2003. To look at Iraqis brought to their knees, scrutinize their faces, admire their resilience. To dream and then return to a heart-wrenching reality. To participate in New York's vague apprehension. To spend an hour at the café. To enter Baghdad and destroy some more houses, raise more dust. To ignore everything about it. To show arrogance, brutality and turn people into beasts for the slaughterhouse. To wish that conquerors be buried in sand.

To program chaos, to make sure that it will be a killer, to prevent a country from being managed decently: that's the day's politics. To pervert language, pervert the children's eyes, corrupt and destroy, that's the new order. To distribute evil with specially built machines. In New York, wait for the rain to stop, there, rain bombs over Baghdad. To define sadness and dissect it in an anatomy course. To catch the flu. To prepare lunch, then go out and contemplate Broadway running down all the way out to the ocean. To buy and buy and return home.

To destroy both the inner and the outer wall. To inhabit the city that has been conquered by murder. To add ruins over ruins. To be jealous of Babylon. To spray hatred on its corpses as well as on the living. To burn live matter. To water the palm trees with fire; that's a barbarian's job. To diagnose madness in those who exterminate Iraq. To not forget the British in this. To not forget, ever. To swear by the mountain and its height that nothing will ever be forgotten. To brand the brain's skin with Inanna's name, to call her to life. To bring her to resurrection. To revive the belief in metempsychosis. To not love. To sleep in order to stay late at night. To discover that the infinitive is a delusion. To lose one's footing.

To walk to the Hudson River. To cross many green lights. To see the sun go down and leave a band of light over the river. To remember the scene as it was, and still is. To wonder subsequently at how the mind created the notion of time when the place did not move. To understand, suddenly, with the suddenness of this same light, that time came out from the triangular confrontation of a place already visited, with the feeling of being actually in it, and with the realization that things aged, and changes occurred in our own body. Memory allows that realization, and the interaction of all these elements with each other creates in our mind the notion—and therefore the nature—of Time.

To keep a distance from desire. To not give up but wait. To exist in doubt, in dark rooms, in the spirit's blackness. To leave, turn left, cross the avenue, enter a supermarket, buy Greek cheese made in Wisconsin . . . linger in front of meat and pineapple, pay for the cheese at the counter, exit, notice that the Twin Towers are missing, try to think of something else . . . To be home.

To keep a benevolent look. To complain about noise. To cry over the sack of Baghdad's archeological museum. To feel pain. To bury love. To spit bitterness. To brush one's teeth. To be sure that the day will look like yesterday. To keep being surprised by the reporters' insensitivity. To throw the paper away. To remember the different wars that wove one's life. To look in one's brain at English soldiers walking in Beirut. To not reach them, because they will remain images. To wash one's hands, dry them. To take a pill. To stare at the curtains. To not sleep during the day.

To dread phone calls. To turn in circles. To watch light's effect on a painting. To think that the tree has grown. Follow sun spots over it. To look through it, and discover a gigantic glass wall. To bring one's glance back the way one brings a boat back to harbor. To compare the ivy to reptiles. To see mirrors. To kill the desire to go out. To count one's days from one morning paper to the next. To feel imprisoned. To forget the world's age but remember one's own. To live off sorrow. To be incapable of laughter.

To wait for the unknown. To not know that Baghdad's National Library has been destroyed. To resent the new

Barbarians. To bleed for each book. To never be able to read one of those books. To plunge into one's veins. To hide into one's brain. To preside over the loss. To observe real endings. To wipe tears. To discover inner tears which turn into wounds. To explore new diseases. To immure oneself in loss. To wallow in dead civilizations, to become one. To bump into the dead. To vomit one's stomach and spit out the heart. To amputate one's head. To agonize on Baghdad's soil. To invoke heat as a weapon. To drink with Michael McClure the blood turned into wine of the Arabs.

To push aside fear. To draw back the curtains. To decide that it's the same. To choose between absolute sorrow, sorrow with no respite, and death. To breathe soot, and uncertainty. To put off all lights and project mental images on the wall. To start a battle to the end. To shift the battle to the next generation. To be aware of the inherent futility of any action. To get out of the house, of the self. To start in the morning the long wait for the night. To make truth explode, to make countries explode. To feel impatient in front of nothingness. To wash one's hands and brush one's teeth.

To notice that mirrors shine during the night and that the mail is waiting to be answered. To worry about the war being waged so far away, so secretly. To already think of the next war. To hammer one's anguish into oneself. To bring about a bird's world in one's imagination. To gaze at the Hudson River through one's eyelashes. To spit pollution. To drive through a green light. To avoid an accident. To become an object. To become the object that that object protects. To hang on nothing. To live with no desires.

To try to be distracted by poetry, by trees. To see the trees grow, in a hurry. To appear and disappear. To take refuge from bestial conquest in false shelters. To chase the refugee, to flush him out of his new refuge. To lodge a bullet in the head and the back of a Palestinian. To add Iraqis to the butchery. To paint big canvases with blood then take a night train, then a plane. To disembark in Paris. To pick up

(115)

the telephone, dial a number in Beirut. To hear the friend say that a Palestinian newsman has been cold-bloodedly shot by some earnest monotheist. To wonder on the necessity of God. To brush the problem aside. To think of Cassandra. To remember the Hammurabi Code. To sink in fat. To look at the narrow and long road that leads the world to the slaughterhouse.

Printed in the USA
CPSIA information can be obtained
at www.ICGtesting.com
JSHW082214140824
68134JS00014B/622